15/8/87.

Make the Most of your
Sewing Machine

Ann Ladbury

Make the Most of your Sewing Machine

B.T. BATSFORD LTD, LONDON

ISBN 0 7134 5159 9

Typeset by Tek-Art Ltd, Kent
and printed in Great Britain by
Butler & Tanner Ltd
Frome, Somerset
for the publishers
B.T. Batsford Limited
4 Fitzhardinge Street
London W1H 0AH

Contents

Acknowledgments

Cynthia Hitchen produced all the decorative designs and all the samples from which the line drawings were done. She also worked very hard seeing how far basic stitches could be extended. Doris Lawrence experimented with literally hundreds of little pieces of fabric to establish the best size of stitch for each. I am enormously grateful to them both for their painstaking assistance. John typed the book on his BBC Microcomputer.

We also extend our thanks to the sewing machine companies who supplied information for the chart on pages 116-119.

Introduction

There are probably few people who really use their sewing machine to its full potential whatever the make or type, whatever the degree of sophistication of the machine or its owner. This is often due to lack of confidence, or not using the machine often enough and therefore forgetting how to use its various functions. It is even possible to forget how to thread it. Blame is often laid on lack of time available but this can be solved in part by keeping the machine handy and not hidden away in the wardrobe – I have even heard the loft referred to as the storage place. Think of your kitchen equipment; the things that have a special place and have plugs on are the ones you use most often.

One of the aims of this book is to present tips and ideas on basic and decorative stitching in order to make machining quicker, more imaginative and more efficient through greater familiarity with the machine. Your sewing will be much more enjoyable. This is not a book about designing nor is it for machine embroiderers.

My own machine is a Pfaff Creative and it is unbelievably versatile. But most of the techniques described in this book can be performed on any machine, however basic.

Whatever machine you have, try to take a broader, more imaginative view of its potential. It takes but a moment to try out a new idea.

The other aim of the book is to show how, with modern machines, we can closely imitate the better aspects of ready-to-wear clothes. Not many years ago we were trying to make clothes with perfect hand stitches and concealed machining. Ready-made clothes feature a variety of interesting techniques and, as domestic sewing machines have advanced alongside industrial ones, we can now achieve similar effects. In fact, interesting, skilful, decorative stitching now brings compliments and you will realise from this book that even a basic zig-zag machine has enormous potential.

This book does not tell you how to thread up and adjust your particular machine; you still need your instruction book for that. *The*

Sewing Machine Handbook by Peter Lucking explains the principles and parts of machines and this book takes up where he leaves off, that is, it covers techniques of sewing on various fabrics. There are hints and tips as well as ideas for simple decoration and I hope it helps you to make more use of your machine.

1

How to use this book

Each chapter deals with a group of fabrics. They are divided according to their handle because it is usually the relative softness, thickness and looseness of weave that determines things like size of stitch, method of neatening etc.

Beneath the main heading is a list of the fabrics in the group from which you can identify the one that you are using. There follow suggestions on appropriate type and size of needle and size of stitch. Seams and hems are mentioned but, in the main, you will need to consult a general sewing book for sewing instructions for collars, pockets, facings etc., *except* where I have a particular tip or piece of advice which applies to a fabric or which uses a particular piece of equipment.

Finally, in each section, you will find suggestions on decorative stitching and designs that you can copy.

Note: Throughout this book metric measurements appear with imperial equivalents in brackets. However, stitch sizes are referred to in mm. throughout. If your machine displays numbers, for instance, 1-5, you can obtain the stitch size suggested by working a few stitches and measuring them with a ruler.

For readers in the United States, products equivalent to those referred to in the text are as follows:

Fold-a-Band   — Waist shaper
Wundaweb   — Save-a-Stitch or Stitch Witchery
Vilene   — Pellon
Stitch-n-Tear — Stitch-n-Tear or WonderUnder
Petersham   — Grosgrain
Bondaweb   — Transfuse

2

Machine Needles

Machine needles are precision-made instruments manufactured to the highest standard of perfection, otherwise they would not perform satisfactorily. Yet, they are undoubtedly the most abused items of sewing equipment. We ignore them, often feed quite the wrong fabric under them and blame them for not stitching correctly when they are old and worn.

Keep plenty of needles; have a stock of all types and all sizes. Get into the habit of using a fresh needle on each new project. Always throw away old or damaged needles. If you stop work on an article and change to a different fabric, remove the needle and put it on one side, stuck into a scrap of that fabric until you are ready to use it again.

It seems fairly obvious that a thick or heavy fabric will require a larger size needle than a thin, fine fabric although not nearly enough people pay enough attention to that fact. A too-small needle will bend and break; too big a needle will make ugly stitches, may not pierce the fabric and will be noisy.

There are different needle-points available for different types of fabrics and using the correct one will ensure a regular stitch that beds into the fabric. The most recent innovation is the one with an elongated scarf which helps to eliminate missed stitches on synthetics. These needles also have a slight ball point and are marked 'Universal' or 'Perfect Stitch'. Other points include Ballpoint for knits and jersey and the spear or wedge point for leather, suede and plastic. The point to use on most modern fabrics is called Regular Sharp.

It is also important to make sure that the range or 'System' marked on the packet is correct for your particular machine. The system number, for example 705H, which is the type for most modern front-bobbin-loading machines, is shown on the packet. Check that you buy the type mentioned in your instruction book especially when buying from a self-service haberdashery stand.

The chart opposite shows the type and size of needle that is correct for various types of fabrics; specific recommendations can be found in the main part of the text.

Fabrics	Size	Point
Fine lightweight woven	70	Regular – sharp point
Medium wovens	90	Regular – sharp point
Heavy wovens	100-110	Regular – sharp point
Light woven synthetics	70	Universal – slight ball
Light jersey	70	Universal – long scarfe
Medium jersey knits	90	Universal – long scarfe
Heavy harsh wovens	90, 100 or 110	Jeans – acute point, long scarfe
Plastic, non wovens	90 or 100	Wedge – spear point

Decorative stitching – all fabrics

For topstitching thread	90, 100, 110, 120	Universal – slight ball, long eye
For twin needle tucks:		
Straight stitching	80, 90, 100	Regular
Zig-zag (set at ½ max width)	80, 90	Regular
For triple needle tucks:		
Straight stitching	80	Regular
Zig-zag (set at ⅓ max width)	80	Regular
For hemstitching:		
Straight stitching	80-100	Wing – blade point
Zig-zag (set at ½ max width)	80	Wing – blade point

N.B.: If your machine takes needles numbered by the old system the equivalents are as follows:

70 = 9, 80 = 11, 90 = 12, 100 = 14, 110 = 16, 120 = 18

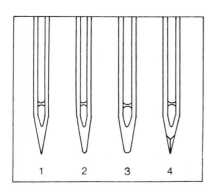

1 *Needle points: (1) Regular sharp point; (2) Universal point; (3) Ballpoint; (4) Wedge or Spear point.*

3

Threads

People so often say 'I've tried lots of different threads and it still won't sew'. This may occasionally be true of old-fashioned straight-stitch machines that baulk at modern threads but modern machines are made to be used with these threads. Or maybe it is the other way round. In any event, the development of both has gone hand in hand in order to satisfy the mass production industry working on all fabrics at unbelievably high speeds and we have benefitted from the production of finer, stronger threads. Problems with the machine are rarely the fault of the thread. It is still important on some fabrics to choose a particular thread but there are other considerations that are often much more important.

Quality

Always buy thread made by one of the major manufacturers. They are the people making threads for industry so it is not only top quality but there is a vast company behind it with laboratories and testing equipment and all that goes with them. You are buying a reliable product but if you do have cause to make a complaint at least it goes to the people who care and who will do something about it. Never be tempted to buy unmarked reels from market stalls. Never buy unnamed thread and never buy in bulk by mail order unless it has a major name on it. These threads may be salvage goods, old, dried-out stock, colours may not be fast etc., in addition these, and cheap threads, very often cause problems with the machine because they are not smooth or uniform in strength.

Economy

Like everything else, thread has increased in price. Poor quality or cheap thread is no economy in the long run because thread is the mainstay of the article being made.

It is more economical to buy big reels. These vary between 250 metres or yards and 1000 metres or yards and although the range of colours is limited, they are the colours that you use most often. There are several ways of preventing thread wastage and if you do a lot of sewing, it is worth getting into the habit of being careful.

Leave short ends only when starting and finishing. Prepare several seams and sew from one to the other, cutting them apart when finished. If a garment has a lining stitched down all round, do not zig-zag any of the raw seam edges. If a garment has a lining which is loose at the hem zig-zag the lower half of the seams only, including lining edges. Neaten raw edges after fitting and marking garment length and then neaten only as far as the hemline, not within it and certainly not the part to be cut off.

Often one row of stitching can secure two layers. For example bias binding can be attached by folding it and enclosing the raw edge of the garment then stitching along the edge but through all layers with a zig-zag stitch. If you do trim off any long ends of thread, use them up for hand sewing.

Colour

The old rule of choosing a shade darker thread for inconspicuous stitching still holds good because the thread on the reel presents a solid block of colour. However, fashion fabrics in the latest colours often precede the addition of new thread colours and you may not be able to match in this way. It is more important to match the general tone and sometimes a lighter shade may match. Also, with fabrics that are not solid dyed there may be a thread colour to match the lighter effect. An example of this sort of fabric is linen, another is jacquard self-colour satin.

It can be difficult to choose thread for fabrics containing a number of colours. The background colour is often not the prominent one and a matching thread may show too much. To make sure the thread will be inconspicuous, place a reel of thread to match each colour in the fabric on the fabric, stand back a few paces and half-close your eyes. The thread you can see most indistinctly will be the best match. Conversely, the one most visible would be suitable for conspicuous topstitching. When selecting thread for topstitching try to avoid white unless the fabric is very white. More subtle shades like ecru, cream and pale beige often look better and don't become grubby.

If using 100 metre or yard reels buy two reels of thread for a garment, three if it is floor length or has a number of seams to be neatened or if the outfit consists of more than one item. Two 100 metre or yard reels will usually make one pair of curtains. Remember that linings and decorative braid, ribbon or trimming should be sewn in thread to match them rather than the garment unless you want a contrasting effect.

Types

There are several types of thread available for use on a machine and for hand sewing.

Core-spun: This is the most modern thread which consists of a spun polyester core providing strength and elasticity, with a covering of cotton yarn which makes it feel soft and pleasant and reduces build-up of static. Use core-spun thread on all fabrics of any fibre or weave. It does not look quite as fine as polyester thread because it is slightly less lustrous. An example of a core-spun thread is Duet.

Spun polyester: This is a pure synthetic thread that is fine, elastic and very strong. It is for machine and hand sewing on all fabrics including those made from natural fibres. It is particularly important to use spun polyester on jersey and stretch fabrics as the thread 'gives' with the seam. Care should be taken not to put a dry iron on hot setting directly on a line of stitching. Polyester fibre shreds, leaving a fine dust on the machine. Get into the habit of using your paint brush to remove it, not only when you see it but also after using pale threads. An example of polyester thread is Drima.

Mercerized cotton: This is traditional, slightly shiny cotton thread. It can be used on all natural woven fabrics although abrasive synthetic fibres have been known to wear through the soft cotton thread. Never use mercerized cotton on jersey, knits or stretch fabrics or any with give in them as the thread will snap in the seams. An example of mercerized cotton is Coats' Super Sheen. It is readily available in size 40 in a very wide range of colours.

Cotton

This is a soft, slightly hairy thread, made in various thicknesses. It is usually only found in black, white and a few colours and often on big reels. It is a basic sewing thread not really suitable for making clothes but is useful for household sewing and repairs. An example of cotton thread is Coats' Chain, available in 100 and 300 metre or yard reels.

Silk

The use and availability of silk thread has diminished somewhat, partly due to the development of modern threads that are finer and cheaper. If you particularly want to sew with silk you will find it is soft and lustrous and makes attractive stitching. An example of silk thread is Faro Seta.

Other threads referred to in this book include variegated threads; metallic threads, both flat and round; twisted with metal yarn such as

Effektgarn; elastic thread for shirring; Coats' Extra-Strong which is a polyester cotton thread used for some heavy fabrics but also for machine decoration. There may be other threads that you wish to use. Always try them out on a scrap of fabric and always adjust the stitch and the tension until the results are acceptable.

Machine Embroidery

These threads are mercerized cotton and are available in size 30 and 50 and sometimes finer. They are fine, twisted and lustrous and are used for all kinds of decorative stitching but will not withstand the strain put on seams. An example of machine embroidery thread is Coats' Anchor.

Quilting thread

Coats' Dual Duty is a fine polyester filament thread that is especially strong to withstand the strain of hand quilting. Although marked 'Hand Quilting Thread' it can be used on a machine and is excellent for all types of decorative stitching as well as basic stitching on fine fabrics.

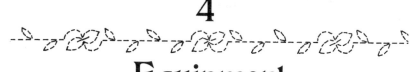

4

Equipment

Some of the following will already be included in your general sewing equipment but some items such as small scissors and a magnetic strip are worth duplicating so that one set is always beside the machine. Keep the following close, beside the machine, on your right.

Scissors

You need small scissors with sharp points for cutting thread, cutting buttonholes, occasionally for snipping fabric. They can also be useful with blades closed, for flattening and dividing gathers as they pass under the foot. Make sure the finger holes of the scissors are large so that you pick them up and put them down quickly. If the holes are small and your fingers stick you will have to stop sewing and use your other hand to ease them off.

Magnetic strip or pin container

Your pin box should be open beside the machine. Better still a flat magnetic strip can rest on the table or, with backing removed, the strip can be stuck to the front or side of the machine.

Bodkin

The point can be used for flattening and for turning collars, belts, tabs, cuffs etc. With most fabrics you will save time by running the point of the bodkin round inside after turning, to push the seam to the edge, you can then flatten it with your fingers, add edge-stitching etc. without pressing with the iron until it is complete.

The Tweezerbodkin is the most useful type as you can remove ends of thread, basting thread, knots etc. with the tweezers end.

Keep the following nearby, in an open box or, better still, in a shallow basket.

Adjustable marker

This short rule with adjustable arrow can be used to check accurate stitch lines, to place seam stitching 1.5cm (⅝in.) from the edge, to check the position of stitching related to particular checks or stripes, and the precise length of darts, buttonholes etc.

Fabric Marking Pen

Use this to indicate precise stopping and starting points; zip and dart ends, alignment positions for braid, pockets, motifs etc. The marks disappear automatically in 1-2 days if you use the 'Fade-Away' pen.

Unpicker

For speed, keep it open and ready to use unless there are children about.

Paper or Stitch-n-Tear

Have small pieces of typing paper or a packet of Stitch-n-Tear ready to place under fine fabrics or for decorative stitching.

Chalk pencil

The best type has a brush on the end. Use for making spot marks on dark fabrics or where fabric pen is unsuitable.

Fray Check

A liquid that is useful on badly fraying fabrics if you are handling a small or fiddly area. A drop or two secures ends of fibre.

Paint brush

Keep a 2cm (¾in.) soft paint brush within reach and use to brush fluff from inside the bobbin area and beneath the needle plate of the machine.

Spare bobbins and feet

Have spare bobbins in the container and also the feet most often used such as those for zips, buttonholes and satin stitch. Others can be kept in the accessory box. Although it is a great help to have an indicator that lights up when the bobbin is nearly empty, it can still be inconvenient to run out of thread in the middle of a line of stitching. Check the thread in the bobbin before starting a long line or a lot of dense stitching.

Needles

Keep packets of standard, ballpoint and universal (scarfe) needles in the container. Keep reserve packets in the accessory box.

Instruction book

Keep the machine manual within reach, together with this book, for quick reference.

Keep the following in the sewing or preparation area:

Ruler and tailor's chalk

Use for ruling straight stitching lines on seams, pleats etc.

Basting tape
Use for anchoring braid etc., or holding down edges and facings, keeping seams or checks matched or use it as double-sided tape for putting in zips.

Wundaweb and Bondaweb
Used in various ways for securing fabric in hems, facings, preventing seam wrinkling, inserting in buttonholes and for appliqué.

Bias Binding Tool
Cut bias strips of fabric as directed on the pack, pass through the tool, press, and they are folded ready for application to edges.

Rouleau needle
For turning narrow tubing, ties, belts etc., right side out. Eliminates broken thread etc.

Large scissors
Not only for cutting out but also for trimming edges after stitching seams and before neatening with zig-zag.

Waste paper bin
Keep a large waste receptacle close beside you, on the right or left depending on which hand you use to discard thread ends etc. In addition, when experimenting on a number of fabrics or when doing a lot of decorative stitching or embroidery have something even closer – tuck a large polythene bag into the top drawer of the cabinet or use a piece of basting tape to attach it to the table edge.

5

The Elements of Good Stitching

Golden rules for using your machine

1   Put in a new needle regularly, say at the start of every two garments. *Throw away the old ones.*

2   Always test the stitch on a scrap of folded fabric and if using interfacing eg. for buttonholes, test the fabric with a layer of interfacing.

3   Always use the same type of thread top and bottom for basic sewing. Remember it looks professional to match a different colour on the bobbin with the underside of the fabric, lining, contrast fabric etc.

4   When working buttonholes always do a trial, cut it and fasten it over the button. On the garment begin with the one that shows least. If you have several to make on a blouse or button-through dress with a narrow wrap, try stitching them diagonally. They then become a feature and they adjust more easily when fastened, keeping the hemline level.

5   Guide the fabric but never push or pull it.

6   If your machine does not have an automatic needle-up facility, always make sure the needle is up before removing fabric.

7   Take care of your machine by keeping it covered when not in use; throw a tea towel over it rather than put it away. Also take care not to chip the machine by careless handling of scissors etc.

8   For safety's sake switch off between sessions of stitching; unplug at the end of the session; switch off when replacing a bulb.

9   Return dials to straight stitch on completing any zig-zag or decorative stitching. On computerized machines this is done by switching off.

10   Press all basic stitching immediately to smooth out wrinkles and embed the thread into the fabric. Some decorative stitching does not require pressing although if it is done on a garment it will have to be pressed at some stage. Cover the board with a towel for raised designs.

6

Understanding Tension

The mention of machine tension makes many people very nervous. It implies that the machine has to be fiddled with and there is a fear that it might never be the same again. Also, the machinist herself will often blame her own shortcomings on the 'tension' without at all knowing why or what it means. I say 'herself' because men don't have this fear of adjusting a machine to make it work properly. I have found that this fear can often be alleviated by a simple explanation. If you do not understand tension read the following.

Two threads are used in machining. One is wound evenly on the bobbin which is placed in the bobbin case or socket. The bobbin must be inserted correctly and the thread pulled around until it slips under a thin piece of metal and emerges from a small hole in the side of the case or socket. The case is inserted in the machine. The top thread is already wound on to a spool when you buy it so it is placed on the machine and passed through the various threading points until it finally goes through the eye of the needle. The bobbin thread is raised so that it emerges through the hole in the needle plate.

Note that with some machines the bobbin is placed directly in the machine. Consult your machine handbook for directions.

The fabric slides under the machine foot but between the two threads. The foot is lowered to grip the fabric. When you start to sew, the teeth below feed the fabric under the foot and if your machine has dual feed, the teeth on top also feed the fabric. The two threads lock to form stitches. The stitch should look similar on both sides of the fabric for basic sewing on seams, hems etc., and for top stitching. Where both sides may possibly be seen, it is essential for the two sides to look the same. If they do not look the same, it means that one or other of the threads is being held too tightly or too loosely at one of the points where it passes through the machine. It is a very simple matter to loosen or tighten each thread until you achieve the correct appearance and this is what is known as adjusting the tension. The illustrations show (a) The

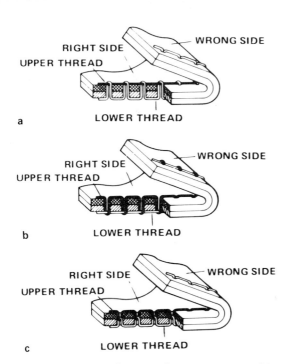

RIGHT SIDE

WRONG SIDE

UPPER THREAD

LOWER THREAD

a

RIGHT SIDE

WRONG SIDE

UPPER THREAD

LOWER THREAD

b

RIGHT SIDE

WRONG SIDE

UPPER THREAD

LOWER THREAD

c

2 *Section through seams showing correct and incorrect tension.*

bobbin thread is looping through the fabric to the surface, the top thread lies on the surface and the bobbin thread is visible too. Either the top is too tight or the bottom too loose. (b) The top thread has been pulled through the lower fabric and is visible. The bobbin thread is lying on the surface. Either the top thread is too loose or the bottom thread too tight. (c) Shows the threads entering on the surface and looping together in the middle of the sandwich of fabric. This is correct because the stitch looks the same on both sides of the fabric.

Adjusting the tension

Check the bobbin thread as follows: Remove the case from the machine, check that the thread is still emerging from the hole correctly, hold the end of the thread and gently bounce the bobbin case like a yo-yo. If the case descends slowly the tension is correct. If it falls to the floor the tension is too loose; if it does not move the tension is too tight. Using your fingernail or the small screwdriver from the machine tool box, loosen or tighten the small screw holding the flat metal spring under which the thread is passed, and turn it *a quarter of a turn only*. Check the thread again. Turn the screw again if necessary. Replace the bobbin case. Test the stitch again. If it is still not correct, adjust the top

21

thread as follows: Tighten or loosen the tension screw or wheel on the upper part of the machine. On modern machines you will find an indicator showing + and − and figures from 0-10. Sometimes the midway point 4-5, which is correct for most fabrics, is marked or shaded. For all general sewing on familiar fabrics, the setting should be in this area. On older machines the spring and the metal discs between which the thread passes are visible. You can watch the discs close up or open up as you adjust the screw – loosen to let more thread through – tighten to keep it back. Exactly the same thing happens on a modern machine but streamlining has resulted in the discs being hidden beneath the surface.

Why adjust tension?

You may be wondering why, if it is so simple, the tension needs to be altered at all?

The locking of the two threads in the middle of the sandwich of fabric is affected by a number of things, the most obvious of which is the thickness of the fabric that you sew on. All modern machines have sensitive tension mechanisms that automatically adjust to a certain extent but you may find you need to help slightly on exceptionally fine, thin, thick or hard fabrics.

Often the construction of the fabric will distort the formation of the stitch. This can sometimes occur with Raschel knit, sweater knits, pile fabrics and those that are thick but loose such as mohair. Slight adjustment of tension will correct the stitch.

Sometimes, with frequent usage, the screw on the spring of the bobbin case accidentally becomes a little looser or tighter than it should be. Sometimes the use of thicker threads will strain the spring. If you cannot adjust it, go to your sewing machine dealer for help. If you use a thick thread or elastic thread or if you use a particularly fine thread you may well have to make a slight tension adjustment. Also, if you sew on single fabric instead of double, the tension may need adjustment. If you sew on very fine or transparent fabric such as chiffon, georgette, net etc., single or double you may have to build up the thickness by putting paper under the seams to make a thicker sandwich before you achieve a satisfactory finish.

Decorative stitching: Including buttonholes, satin stitch, etc. When sewing buttonholes you should make sure of a good effect by adjusting the tension slightly so that the top thread passes a little further to the underside. On some machines this is achieved by threading through an extra hole in the bobbin case to tighten the bottom thread slightly. On others, the top tension should be loosened.

When working satin stitch on the upper side of the fabric, the top tension should be slightly loosened for the same reason.

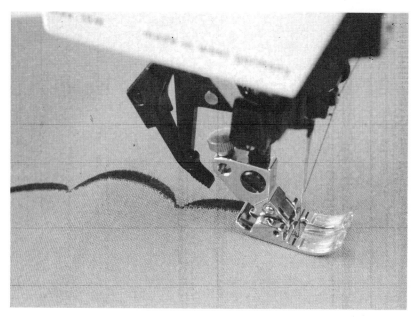

3   *Satin stitch scallops.*

If you are using a different thread, top and bottom, either for a particular colour effect or for heavy top stitching, couching, metal thread and other decorative work then quite obviously the tension of one or both threads must be adjusted to cope with the varying thickness.

In the same way if you are stitching from the underside of the fabric in order to achieve a particular effect on the right side, the tension should be adjusted to make sure only one thread is visible on the right side.

When doing decorative work on a single layer of fabric there are very few occasions when you will not have to place a layer of paper or Stitch-n-Tear beneath your fabric to support it. In fact fine or transparent fabrics may require two layers. Remember to re-adjust the screw on the bobbin case for basic sewing.

Spare bobbin case: If you habitually use thick threads or metal or elastic threads in your bobbin or, if you don't at present, but find you want to after reading this book, it is best to go to your sewing machine dealer and buy an extra bobbin case. Loosen the screw on it a little, mark it with nail varnish on the end of the *latch* only and keep it for thick thread. This ensures that you can do basic sewing at any time without finding you have forgotten to tighten up the screw.

Occasional stitch distortion: If you test your fabric and achieve the correct stitch as described, it will remain constant unless one of the following things happen accidentally or if in haste you failed to thread up the machine correctly. Most faults or impending faults can be *heard*. Once you are familiar with your machine you will recognise any change of tone.

Stitch distortion, breaking thread, failure to stitch or sudden change in tension will be due to one of the following:

1. Uneven winding of thread on bobbin.

2   Top thread caught on notch or label on thread reel.

3   Lump or knot in thread as it approaches the eye of the needle.

4   Bottom thread caught under spring in case or round central spindle.

5   The wrong make of bobbin is being used. (This can happen at classes.)

6   Accumulated fluff and lint, usually from just beneath the hole in the needle plate, gets sewn in with the stitch.

7   Static build-up when using synthetic thread on very static fabric such as synthetic jersey.

8   Needle hits a pin or a knot of basting thread.

9   Needle is blunt, or bent, or the wrong size or type for the fabric.

10   Poor quality or old thread.

11   Thread not the same top and bottom but tension not adjusted.

12   You started carelessly, without ensuring both threads were held out behind the foot and the bottom thread tangled. If you have a problem, unthread the machine, top and bottom, and remove the bobbin. Cut off the ends of thread.

13   Fabric jams into hole in needle plate due to starting off without the foot completely on the fabric or failure to use ballpoint needle on pliable fabric such as knit. Brush out fluff. Re-thread the machine with more care. Test the stitch. In most cases this will cure it. If not, unthread the needle and insert a new one, *throwing away* the old one.

If you still have a problem, try stitching on a double layer of a basic medium-thickness cotton fabric and if the stitch looks correct on it, return to your problem fabric and adjust stitch size and type, needle size and type, tension and possibly thread type until it too is correct.

It is doubtful you will still have a problem after this but if you have, call in an experienced friend to check what you are doing. If he or she cannot solve it, take the machine to your dealer.

7

Supporting the Fabric for Machining

Fabric sometimes requires some support underneath in order to produce even stitching, to eliminate missed stitches, to prevent the fabric from being pushed down into the needle hole or, with decorative stitching, to throw the decoration into relief and raise it. There are various methods to choose from, depending on the fabric and the stitching.

If the support can be left in position after stitching, use Light weight sew-in Vilene or Ultra Soft iron-on Vilene. For slight support in seams on lightweight fabric or in small areas, place one or possibly two layers of tissue paper under the fabric. To support stitching on a single layer of fabric use typing paper. Paper must be removed after stitching by gently easing it away taking great care not to distort or even break the stitches. The firmest support of all is Stitch-n-Tear, a papery non-woven sheet. This can be used beneath all types of stitching on all fabrics. It can be gently removed afterwards, larger pieces being kept for future use. If it is inadvisable to use any of these materials, for example on loosely constructed cloth such as hessian, the fabric itself can be stiffened with an application of wallpaper paste. Spread out the fabric to dry, pulling it to shape and if required for the decoration to be worked, you can move some of the yarns or make holes with a bodkin while the fabric is wet. Less drastic alternatives for lighter fabrics and in smaller areas include an application of Fray Check or a mixture of six parts of acetone to one part colourless nail varnish. The simplest thing is to add the acetone to an almost empty varnish bottle, shake well and apply to the fabric using the brush in the bottle.

Advice for Beginners

If you have never before used a sewing machine you must first learn how to control it; to sew straight lines, corners, circles etc., and only then how to thread it, in that order. Unfortunately it is like most things, the only way to master the basic skill is to indulge in some boring practice. But it is like riding a bicycle, you never lose the knack once you have learnt it. At least today's beginners don't have to start by learning to work the treadle.

Spend as much time as you can sitting at the machine practising. Do not thread it, simply stitch on paper working through the following exercises. At the end you will be automatically stopping correctly and reaching for the right controls. In fact most activities will be familiar but in addition you will have seen how fabric is fed, how the feed teeth work, various sizes and types of stitch in reverse, in zig-zag and in trimotion. After this, thread the machine following the instructions in the handbook and start practising· on fabric. Check material, such as gingham, is useful for this. Always use it folded double. Work through the exercises again, this time concentrating on inserting the fabric carefully, stopping with the needle up every time and removing work correctly. Also try adjusting the top tension control slightly so that you can observe the effect and start to learn something about stitch tension.

Practise on paper (machine not threaded but needle inserted).

a) Slide a piece of plain paper under the foot, use the lever to lower the presser foot and machine to the opposite edge of the paper. Raise the needle if your machine has no needle-up/down facility.

b) Slide the paper under the foot until the edge is level with the back of the foot. Lower the foot, machine to the opposite edge stopping with the needle up precisely at the edge of the paper. Raise foot, remove paper. Repeat several times. On the final row, go into reverse for 5mm (¼in.) at the start and finish of the row.

c) Repeat b) on lined paper until you can keep straight.

d) Rule several corners or use squared paper and work up to the corner, stop with needle *down*, raise foot. Swivel paper to correct position, lower foot, work on. Repeat at least 6 times. Set your machine to stop at needle-down if you can, before you start.

e) On plain paper mark pairs of pencil dots varying distances apart and work rows between the dots, starting and stopping *exactly* on each dot.

f) On plain paper use pencil dots to outline simple shapes made up of straight lines such as house, triangle, square, hexagon etc. Work round each one.

g) On plain paper work a number of straight lines but alter the controls for each one, working through various lengths of straight stitch, various lengths and widths of zig-zag and some open decorative stitches (not satin stitch).

h) On plain paper draw a circle, outlining a saucer or dish, and work round it to get the feel of easing round a curve.

i) Draw several concentric circles and work round each, starting with the outer one and making sure the stitching (holes) of each joins up but does not overlap.

j) On plain paper draw a continuous circular line – a spiral. Start at the outside and work round and round to the centre.

k) Using a small dish or saucer or even a coin, outline a row of half-circles to make scallops; join them with a straight line 5mm (¼in.) long. Work round the scallops.

Repeat the above exercises on fabric but if you have a chance to stitch on an article instead of a sample, do so and skip the routine practice.

Note that quite young children can do the paper exercises and derive a lot of enjoyment from it.

9

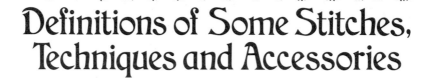

Definitions of Some Stitches, Techniques and Accessories

Automatic stitches

Stitches that are produced by touching a button, depressing a switch, turning a dial or inserting a pattern cam in the machine. On most machines you can then adjust the length and width until you obtain the result you want.

Balance wheel

The small solid wheel at the right of the machine. It rotates when you sew. On basic machines it is used to raise or lower the needle, the centre part being used to disengage the needle movement in order to wind a bobbin.

Basting

This is an extra long, straight stitch and the method of achieving it varies with the type of machine. On some machines, you simply need to alter the indicator, no other adjustment being necessary. On others you may find instructions in the manual for using a basting needle; which has two eyes. Another method can be employed on all machines but it requires care and control and it is to drop the feed teeth and move the fabric through evenly, with stitch length 0 and making stitches as long as required. Sew very slowly, one stitch at a time and hold the fabric taut.

Binding foot

A foot consisting of a tube of thin metal into which pre-folded bias binding is fed. The fabric is fed into a slot on the left. The binding must be the correct width for the foot otherwise stitches will not fall on the binding.

4 *Basting and top stitching.*

Blind hemming

A method of machining hems but without any stitching being visible on the outside of the garment. A special foot is required which guides the fabric, and the machine must be set to the blind hemstitch which makes two or three straight stitches and one zig-zag to the left. On some machines the same foot can be used for applying piping.

Buttonhole foot

Some machines require an attachment for making buttonholes but modern machines have buttonholing as a built-in facility and it is welcomed with relief by everyone. The operation of the buttonhole becomes simpler with each grade of machine. With basic machines the bars are stitched forward only so the fabric has to be turned to work the second side. The buttonhole must be very accurately marked with fabric pen. On other machines a dial is turned but not the fabric. Most modern machines have a scaled buttonhole foot to make it easier to make them even-sized but the computer machines will automatically

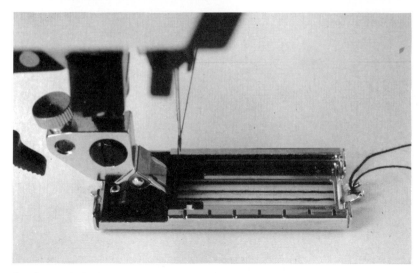

5 *Buttonhole foot with gimp or filling cord in position.*

produce as many as you want to the size of the first one you do. Always practise to get the correct size, cutting it and fastening it over a button to check it.

Drop Feed

Machines vary in the way this is done. On most machines the feed teeth are lowered by turning a control, others have a plate supplied with them that is attached to the machine to cover the teeth. In both cases the teeth do not operate and so the machinist has to control the movement of the fabric. The advantage of being able to do this is that free patterning including repairs, can be worked to any size and design, with a higher density of stitching in some places if required. Stitching is sometimes done without a foot. Fabric usually has to be put in a hoop to hold it taut for drop-feed stitching. Two hands are needed to control the fabric so it cannot be done on a hand machine. Always lower the presser foot lever even if no sewing foot is attached. Make sure dual feed is disengaged.

Dual feed

This is probably the most important recent development as far as the home sewer is concerned, eliminating an age-old problem. As the term suggests, the layers of fabric are fed under the needle evenly. On some machines this is done by attaching what is described as a 'walking' foot each time it is required but undoubtedly the superior version is the one

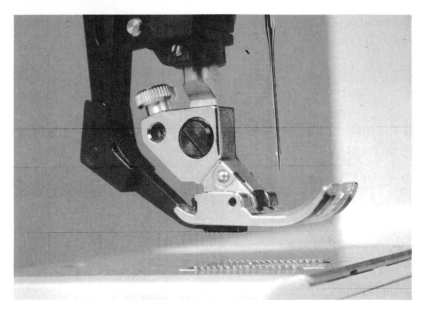

6 *Dual feed engaged.*

that is built in. The dual feed claws the upper layer of fabric through in the same way that the feed teeth claw at the lower layer so there is never a piece left over at the end of a seam which has to be cut off. Patterns can be perfectly matched and will remain matched including checks, stripes, plaids and florals; seams will not cockle one side even on long dresses or curtains; velvet and pile fabric will not creep and pucker; fine fabrics will not wrinkle where the lower feed teeth pierce them; even attaching braid and ribbon is easier because the usual result of tight braid and wrinkled fabric is eliminated.

Embroidery hoop

This is essential for drop-feed stitching and free embroidery as it holds the fabric taut. The inner ring must be covered to stop the fabric slipping and to prevent marks being made on the fabric. Bind the ring evenly and tightly, using tape or bias binding opened out flat, strips of thin fabric cut on the cross or narrow bandage. Fabric must be put in the hoop so that the underside is flat on the machine bed and the side on which you will stitch is inside the hoop but at the bottom (unlike hand embroidery where the hoop is held the other way up). Use the darning foot or for better visibility, no foot. Occasionally, the regular sewing foot is used. Hoop may have a section cut away but if not, remove foot, drop the feed, insert hoop, replace foot.

Even feed

See Dual Feed.

Feed teeth

The serrated metal beneath the foot, set into the plate, which grip the fabric and move it under the foot towards the back.

Fringing foot

Available for most modern machines, this foot has a raised bar in the centre which lifts the top thread. Used with a long stitch it makes tailor tacking tufts; closed up, it forms fringing or chenille loops.

Gathering foot

A simple attachment which slightly gathers the under layer and stitches the seam in one go. Practise on measured spare fabric and calculate how much longer the bottom fabric needs to be. Slightly stretch the upper fabric as you sew.

Machine bed

Usually taken to mean the remainder of the flat sewing area excluding or including the needle plate.

Needle holder (needle bar)

The vertical metal bar into which the needle is inserted, it being held in place by means of a screw.

Needle plate

Smooth metal plate under the foot containing the hole for the needle and also the feed teeth.

Needle threader

An excellent built-in facility on some machines and another that is welcomed by everyone, not just because up to now the light on the machine has never been positioned to throw light on the eye of the needle, but also because the cut end of synthetic thread cannot be flattened to make threading easy. If you haven't a built-in needle threader keep one of the little wire threaders by the machine, or attached to it on a piece of thread.

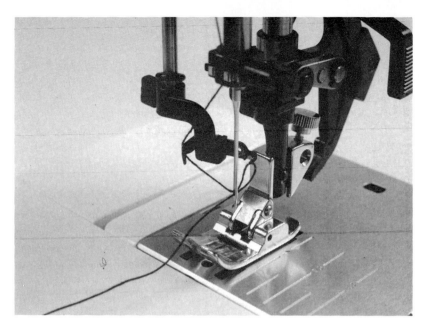

7 *Automatic needle threader.*

Pin-tucking feet

Very fine tucks that can be made by folding fabric right side out, pressing a crease on the straight grain and working a straight or zig-zag stitch along the fold. The quantity worked and the distance between them varies according to the fabric and the effect required. A more defined result is achieved if the tucks are corded. A much easier way to pin tuck is to attach a grooved foot to the machine. This is often purchased as an additional accessory and is used with a twin needle.

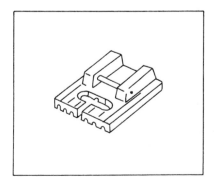

8 *Grooved foot for pin-tucking.*

Most makes of machine provide several feet for tucking, each with a different number of grooves, 3, 5, 7, even 9, which vary in width according to the thickness of the fabric. For instance, a foot with only 3 grooves obviously means the grooves are wider and so it is for use on thick fabric. The choice of size of twin needle must be correct as the distance between the needles must correspond with the width of the groove. It follows that the thickness of cord must also be varied as follows:

| No. of Grooves | Twin Needle | | Cord | Stitch length straight |
	Size mm	Space mm		
9	80	1.6	Topstitching thread or none.	2.5
7	80	2.0	1 thickness fine crochet cotton.	2.5
5	90	2.5/3.0	2 thicknesses fine crochet cotton or thicker cotton.	2.5
3	90/100	4.0	Quilting wool, or other thick yarn.	3.0

N.B.: Equivalent sizes for old machine needles are as follows: 80 = 11, 90 = 12, 100 = 14

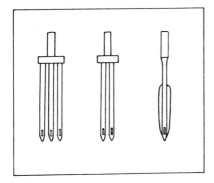

9 *Specialist needles, L to R: Triple needle; Twin needle; Wing or Spear point.*

Use sewing thread top and bottom, a straight stitch and tighten the top tension. Thread the cord up through the hole under the foot and pass end under foot to the back. Machines without a hole may have an attachment for holding the cord in front of the foot. Alternatively cut a short piece of the outer casing of electric cable, thread the end of the cord through and sellotape the cable to the machine. Tucks can then be stitched without a guide but you would have to make sure it remained in position underneath the fabric. Always clean under the needle plate as cord passing through the hole will pull lint and fluff up with it.

Presser foot

This is the sewing foot in use, whether you have the regular foot on or a special attachment. The presser foot lever is the lever at the side or back used for raising and lowering the foot.

Roller foot

This is for use on leather, suede fabric, plastic, PVC and other fabrics that are inclined to stick or feed unevenly. Alternatively, a Teflon-coated foot is effective if one is available for your particular machine.

Ruffler

Sometimes called a pleating attachment, this is a cumbersome but very effective foot for attaching to basic machines or older models. It can be adjusted to make pleats of varying depths. Fabric can be gathered alone or joined to another layer at the same time. Practise on measured fabric and calculate what length will be required.

Straight stitching

This is a lock-stitch formed when upper and lower threads loop together in the fabric. All machines of any type or age have this as the basic stitch, excluding overlocking or serging machines.

Straight stitching is used for joining seams, adjusted to a length that looks right on the fabric, for decorative stitching and for basting, gathering, top-stitching, stay-stitching, double thread stitching, twin and triple needle sewing, darning, quilting and free embroidery.

Take-up lever

The shaped hook either with a slot or a hole in the end which holds the thread. The lever, now largely concealed by the machine's casing, moves up and down as each stitch is formed.

Teflon-coated foot

If these are available for your machine they are useful for stitching on difficult fabrics such as leather and plastic, suede fabric and synthetics which build up static and cause missed stitches.

Trimotion stitches

These are automatic stitches that operate in three directions, forward, backward, and side to side in variation. Their development has made possible the jersey, stretch and pullover range of stitches as well as elaborate decorative ones including, on some machines, complete motifs, monograms etc.

Walking foot

See Dual Feed.

Zig-zag stitching

Domestic machines were revolutionised when the sideways needle movement was introduced. Some early machines were referred to as swing-needle models to distinguish them from straight stitch machines. A basic zig-zag stitch can be used decoratively and for neatening raw edges and it has many other uses such as for attaching braid and ribbon. However, from basic zig-zag many other sewing jobs are possible, including buttonholes (satin stitch is closed-up zig-zag), blind hemstitch and many others that combine straight and sideways movements of the needle. The maximum width of stitch varies slightly between models but is usually around 5-6mm (¼in.).

Turning a corner

In sheer and lightweight fabrics stitch up to the corner and stop with the needle down in the fabric. Set your machine to needle/down if you can, before you begin. Raise the presser foot, swivel the work to the new position, lower the foot and continue stitching.

In medium thickness fabrics, stitch almost to the corner, stop with the needle down, lift the foot and swivel the work far enough to take one stitch diagonally across the corner, swivel again and proceed. If the fabric is bulky use the same method but take three stitches to turn the corner, each one angled slightly more until the corner is complete.

Raw edges of all corners must be trimmed close to the stitching first across the corner and then again. Turn the fabric right side out by placing your thumb inside and snapping the upper layer over it. Use the point of a bodkin to gently ease out the corner, twisting the point rather than pushing it. If the fabric frays, push in a small piece of Wundaweb; it will melt when pressed and reinforce the fraying fibres. Roll and press the corner carefully. If you baste the edge before pressing, remember not to take a stitch through the Wundaweb. In some cases the corner may be stitched a second time but this can make it rather stiff.

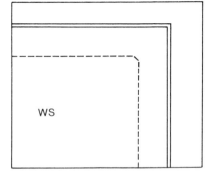

WS

10 *Turning a corner.*

10

Stitching and Decorating Fabric

Group One: Fine mesh fabrics

Net, tulle, veiling, fine lace with net ground, raschel net, transparent tricot, embroidery net.

Due to the open construction, these fabrics are difficult to hand-baste and pins tend to wobble. They are all completely transparent and soft. If part of the garment needs supporting or interfacing, use plain net. Knits and tricot curl up but none of the fabrics in this group will fray.

Needle – 70 Regular. Many are easier to sew if Ballpoint is used. On some machines if regular needle is used paper will be needed beneath fabric.

Stitch – Straight: 2mm. Zig-zag: 2mm wide, 1.5mm long. [Refer to note on stitch sizes on page 11 if your machine shows numbers rather than metric sizes.]

Thread – Polyester for basic stitching. Machine embroidery for decoration.

Seams – Narrow: one row of close overlock or similar or one row straight or slight zig-zag, edge trimmed then small zig-zag or overlock over both edges together. Machine fell seam: if suitable garment (it is visible). French seam: may be suitable but as all fabrics are springy may be too bulky. Overlap: the best choice for figured or patterned lace and for some raschel type fabrics. Lap one edge over the other, matching seam allowances and pin across the seam. Using a small zig-zag and matching thread stitch the seam, right side up, following the outline of the motifs as far as possible, moving from one to the other with a straight line. Carefully trim both raw edges close to zig-zag. Press.

Hems and edges – Narrow: fold up once and zig-zag, blind stitch or use running zig-zag or similar. Edge stitch: Fold up once and work small zig-zag on fold. Trim away excess. Shell edge: fold up once and work medium width blind-hem or zig-zag so that needle clears the fold when it swings to the right. Adjust tension if necessary to make thread draw in the folded edge. Deep hem on lace etc.: face with net. Bound: use strips of solid fabric passed through a bias tool and pressed, or use bought satin binding. Wrap over edge of fabric, attach with medium width zig-zag or decorative stitch.

* Stitch all hems with right side up.
* Use two rows of straight stitch to gather; one row tends to make bulges.
* It is very unlikely that you will be able to use the hemming foot on these fabrics.

Free design on net
Zig-zag or straight stitch

Delicate free-style designs can be worked with net in hoop and drop-feed. It helps to have net double, cutting away one layer after main motifs are stitched. Plan a leaf or petal design and mark a few guide points using fabric pen. Drop the feed, insert hoop, attach darning foot or use no foot at all. Attach extension to provide maximum flat working area.

Stitch with a very small zig-zag, very small straight stitch, or very wide zig-zag. All these produce different effects and the speed of sewing will also make the stitch different. A further variation is straight stitch with very loose bottom tension so that bottom thread comes to the surface in rings.

Twin needle on tricot – Suitable for nightwear, lingerie and baby clothes. Best effects obtained with matching or toning thread. Do not use cord.

Hems – Fold up fabric once on to wrong side to a depth of 1-3cm (³⁄₈in.-1¹⁄₄in.) and stitch with small gap twin needle, regular foot, fabric right side up, below raw edge which can be seen through upper layer. On wrong side trim away excess.

Free design – Use two layers of fabric, mark main points of leaf or stylised flower design, and stitch. Paper may be needed underneath. An

11   *Free design on net.*

attractive effect can be obtained with zig-zag stitch and loose top tension.

Lace appliqué – Motifs can be cut from lace and applied to net, veiling etc. Back the piece of lace with Bondaweb, peel off the paper backing, cut out motifs and place in position on base fabric. Press to secure.

   * If supporting transparent fabric with paper or Stitch-n-Tear, mark the design on that instead of the fabric.

Automatic scallops – Satin stitch – If your machine has built-in stitches this is probably the most satisfactory and the most professional edge finish for most mesh fabrics. It is too stiff for tricot. Using mercerized thread and the satin stitch foot, place Stitch-n-Tear or typing paper under fabric, trimming smoothly the edge to be followed. Scallops look better if fine crochet cotton is inserted but this may be difficult to do unless you have the type of foot with the hole in the front for threading the cord. If you do not use cord, adjust the tension and stitch length to compensate. Carefully snip away excess fabric after stitching, although, on net, you will find that it has all been drawn in.

   * Try gold or silver thread wound on the bobbin, loosen bottom tension and stitch from the wrong side.

Corded hem
Zig-zag stitch

Suitable for transparent fabrics, edges of net curtains, dress frills etc., using a fine crochet cotton to match or tone with the fabric; place it on the hem line, inside the raw edge, on the right side of the fabric. Use a small zig-zag stitch and sew over the cord. Trim off the surplus fabric close to the stitching.

Zig-zagging edges
For a smooth start and correctly positioned, even stitching, begin by lowering the needle into the hole, butt the fabric up against it on the left and begin stitching.

Joining elastic
Hold the two ends together and stitch across using a large zig-zag. Make another row 1cm (³⁄₈in.) away in case the elastic is too tight and the first row has to be undone.

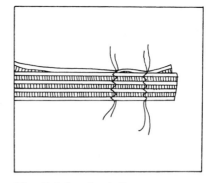

12 *Joining elastic for easy adjustment.*

Group Two: Soft, transparent fabrics

Polyester chiffon, silk chiffon, georgette

These are probably the softest, finest fabrics you will ever handle and for most people they are the most difficult. They are slippery and fray badly and they are so fine that it is not always easy to achieve a good machine stitch. The fabrics are shown to best advantage if a lot of fabric is used in gathers etc., or if small amounts are used in such things as scarves and bows. Garments require an under layer; sometimes two layers of fabric can be used in certain areas to make it more opaque. Two layers together are easier to stitch.

Needle – 70

Stitch – Straight: 1.5mm long. Zig-zag: 2.5mm wide, 1.5mm long.

Thread – Polyester or mercerized.

Seams – French: finished width no more than 3-4mm (⅛in.). The fabric will slip under the foot so it is difficult to keep seams an even width. Narrow: work a very narrow zig-zag over a row of straight stitching 3mm (⅛in.) away from the seam stitching.

Hems and edges – Rolled hem: work a row of straight stitching on the hemline. Trim surplus fabric close to stitching. Roll hem and straight stitch or zig-zag, the initial stitching providing a firm edge to roll as you stitch. Do not baste a rolled hem. Shell hem: using the blind hemstitch or similar, stitch a narrow pre-basted hem so that the zig-zag thrown to the side just misses the fold. Double bind: cut bias strips of fabric 2.5cm (1in.) wide, fold wrong side inside and press. Stitch on to wrong side of garment with all raw edges level and taking 3mm (⅛in.) seam allowance. Roll binding firmly to the right side until the fold barely covers the stitching. Hold it in place with a very small zig-zag stitch or with a decorative stitch set to the full width of the binding.

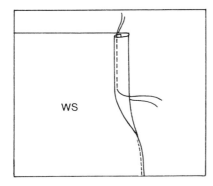

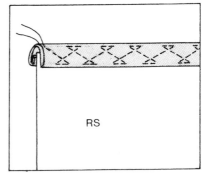

13 *Rolled hem secured with straight stitch.*

14 *Double binding finished on right side with decorative stitch.*

Garments can be lined to the edge but they should not have the edges finished with shaped facings which are totally visible.

Deep hem: if the garment edge is fairly straight, an attractive deep shadow hem can be made. It adds weight to a dress, jacket, negligee etc., in any of the fabrics in this group. It is not suitable for a flared hem because the fullness in the part that is turned up would be visible on the outside.

Turn up and baste and press the hem. Do not trim it to depth but, on the outside, mark a line of dots using fabric pen at an even depth of 3-5mm (⅛in.-¼in.). Select a decorative stitch such as scallop and set fairly close but not at satin stitch. Use either a perfectly matching thread or a paler shade than the fabric and stitch along the marked line with the fabric right side up and having tissue paper or Stitch-n-Tear underneath it. Make sure the pattern matches at the end of the line by gently pulling the fabric to lengthen the final stitches. On the wrong side gently ease away the paper. Remove the excess fabric by carefully trimming close to the stitching.

Twin needle shadow patterns

A very attractive but subtle form of decoration that can be applied to plain and patterned transparent fabrics in pale colours. The complexity of design is a matter of choice but the simpler the outline, the easier it is. Also there is less risk of the fabric wrinkling or even snagging.

Plan a simple, non-symmetrical motif for a blouse pocket, the back of a negligee, the points of a collar, or plan to do a border parallel with a hem, each side of a blouse fastening or along a yoke edge. The decoration must be worked before assembling the garment except in the case of a hemline where it will help to stitch up the main seams first.

Find a piece of fabric of the same type as the garment but a little darker in colour or a contrast. Alternatively, a piece of the garment fabric can be used although the result is less interesting. Baste the

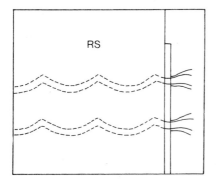

RS

15 *Twin needle shadow scallops on soft transparent fabric*

contrast fabric under the garment fabric. On the right side mark out the outline to be followed using fabric pen or chalk or pencil. If you intend to work parallel lines such as the scallops shown in the illustration, mark one line only and use the machine foot to guide you when stitching the second line.

Insert a twin needle size 1.6 in the machine, use a small, straight stitch and thread to match either the upper or lower fabric and sew along the outline. Remember that it is very tricky to turn corners neatly with a twin needle; it is wiser to keep to curved designs. You may need to loosen the top tension a little and you may need paper underneath the fabric. On completion, carefully ease away the paper and trim the excess fabric close to the stitching.

Stitching a collar

If the pattern provides the complete collar and not just half and if you are sure you will not be using the pattern again, a collar can be made quickly and accurately as follows: cut out collar in appropriate weight of iron-on Vilene and press it to wrong side of fabric, lining up straight grain as indicated on pattern. Place another piece of fabric right side down on right side of interfaced piece, matching straight grain. Secure with 3 pins down the centre. Turn fabric over and cut out collar following edge of interfacing. Place collar pattern on top, matching edges and replace the 3 pins through all layers. Baste round outer edge of collar through pattern and fabric inside seam line without pulling stitches tight, or insert a few more pins, well within seam line. Stitch outer edge of collar following printed seam line. Tear paper away and trim and turn collar in the usual way.

If the pattern has no printed seam line draw one, measuring 1.5cm (5/8in.) accurately from

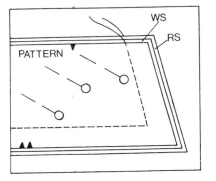

16   *Stitch through pattern, along printed seam line, for perfect collar points.*

edge of paper.

If you think you will need the pattern again make a copy of it first, but for accuracy use the tissue version to stitch through. Alternatively remove main part of tissue carefully after stitching, pin or stick to new paper and add the seam allowance before putting it away for future use.

If you are using a pattern that has no seam edge on the paper, make a copy in tissue paper, adding the seam. It does not work to stitch beside the edge of the paper as it moves too much.

Group Three: Crisp, transparent fabrics

Organdie, organza, flock nylon, plain and figured silk organza.

Although fine, these fabrics are springy and because they are woven from filament yarns, they will fray. It is also difficult to press edges and seams flat. The silk fabrics will usually be easier to handle than the synthetics.

Needle – 70 Regular.

Stitch – Straight: 1.5mm long. Zig-zag: 2.5mm wide, 1.5mm long.

Thread – Polyester for basic stitching, machine embroidery decoration.

Seams – Hairline: row of straight stitching with small zig-zag over the top after trimming. French: can be used if fabric frays badly but makes garment stick out as seams will not lie flat. Very thin, transparent fabric may need paper underneath.

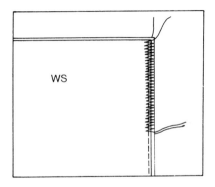

17 *Hairline seam for transparent fabrics.*

Hems and edges – Narrow: finished with small zig-zag or twin needle. Rolled: using hemming foot. Both straight and shell edge are suitable. Hairline: fold edge under once, work very small zig-zag over fold. Trim away excess on wrong side.

   * Avoid deep double-fold hems where possible. If they must be made, for example on children's clothes, stitch with decorative stitch or attach ribbon to outside.

   * On striped or check fabric make a deep hem the width of a stripe and stitch with very small zig-zag in thread to match heavier yarn of fabric.

   * Avoid facings.

   * Use machine embroidery thread for buttonholes.

Pin-tucks
Straight stitch; Tucking Foot.

Use a 9-groove foot, narrow twin needle, and top stitch thread as filling cord. Thread the machine with two reels of matching or toning mercerized thread. Crease fabric for first line or make row of dots with fabric pen and stitch one tuck, fabric right side up. Move fabric and lower the foot so that the tuck fits into the next groove but one. Continue in this way making parallel tucks. On some fabrics every groove can be used but it makes the area stiff and could only be done for a yoke or cuffs, not for an area required to hang.

   * Prevent pin-tucked hems from curling up by catching the hem with two tucks, then trimming away excess fabric but continuing with the pin-tucks above the hem.

Buttonholes
Follow the instructions in the handbook for attaching foot and stitching. Some machines offer both narrow and wide beads, others have a built-in keyhole buttonhole as well as basic bar-tack variety. Whatever your machine does you still have to operate it. Remember to always sew on a double layer of fabric, adding an extra piece of lining or cotton if necessary. In most places there will also already be a layer of Vilene or other interfacing. It may help to put Stitch-n-Tear under fine fabrics. It helps prevent fraying if you put Wundaweb between the layers. Mark the buttonhole positions with tacks, fabric pen, chalk pencil or tailor's chalk. On very fine fabrics stitch round once using machine embroidery thread; on lightweight fabrics use the same thread and stitch round twice. On medium fabrics use polyester or mercerized thread. On heavy fabrics put a filler cord in the edge.

Understitching
This is a line of stitching that may be placed close to a garment edge but through the facing and seam allowances only. I am personally against under-stitching because I see it as a lazy way of making a facing lie flat instead of properly rolling, basting and pressing it flat. In addition, there is no doubt that because the stitching is placed on the facing and it clamps two lots of seam allowance to it, the facing is made heavier and stiffer and it then tends to pop out of position.

   However, for those that haven't time to roll edges, open out the garment with facing extended and place under the machine right side up. Push the seam allowances under the facing and stitch close beside the seam line. Using both hands pull both garment and facing outwards from the foot to avoid wrinkles. Use a small neat stitch and perfectly matching thread as the stitching will show in wear.

Group Four: Crisp, close, twill weave fabrics

All types of satin including those made from silk, acetate, viscose or polyester yarns.

Twill weaving with slippery yarns produces fabrics that are shiny on the right side. If crêped yarns are used, the reverse side of the fabric is matt and this side can be used as the right side if preferred, often as trimming. All these fabrics fray badly and some crease very badly which tends to be more obvious on plain colours because the surface is shiny.

Needle – 70; 90 on heavy satin. Regular needle although if problems are experienced with the finer fabrics use Universal (scarfe).

Stitch – Straight: 1.5mm long. Zig-zag: 2mm wide, 1.5mm long.

Thread – Polyester. Machine embroidery for decoration.

Seams – Narrow: straight stitch, then zig-zag both edges to neaten after trimming. French: use on soft silks only. Width 5mm (¼in.). Open: difficult to press flat without getting iron marks. Seams tend to pucker on the straight grain which is more obvious on plain pale colours. Dual feed is a great help here.

Hems and edges – Wundaweb: use on heavy and crisp satins. Neaten edge, fold 3cm (1¼in.) on to wrong side, press, insert Wundaweb. Press again but not over the neatening. On long skirts, wedding dresses etc., make hem 6cm (2½in.) deep and use 2 widths of Wundaweb. May also need strip of Vilene to stiffen. Narrow rolled: soft satins can be rolled with hemming foot, either plain or shell hem. Narrow decorative: edges of frills etc., can be finished with narrow hem folded over twice and stitched with a pattern; length ½-1; width 4. Bound: bind narrowly with self fabric (not heavy satins) or use bought satin binding although this will stiffen the edge. Facings: use lining fabric or net on heavy satin to avoid bulky edges.

Motif quilting
Straight stitch

An attractive way of breaking up the shine of plain satin. Plan a geometric design that can be extended if necessary. Can be used on collars, particularly shawl collars, cuffs, pocket tops, bodice panels, trouser hems.

Baste a layer of thin wadding on to the wrong side of the fabric before cutting out the garment section. Mark the outline of the garment. You may be able to back the wadding with a layer of self fabric or lining. For instance, cut deep trouser hems and fold up before quilting; pocket can have lining attached; bodice could have facing extending over quilted area. If you cannot do this, baste a piece of muslin over the wadding. It is much easier to quilt with the right side up and now that we have marking pens it is possible to mark out a design with dots. Alternatively, mark the design on the backing fabric and stitch from the wrong side.

Attach quilting foot. Straight stitch length 3mm (⅛in.). Use sewing thread. Loosen tension of thread that will be on right side of garment. Sew design avoiding overlapping ends of stitching. On completion, pull thread ends to wrong side and tie off. Add single motif embroidery.

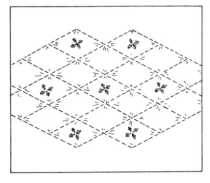

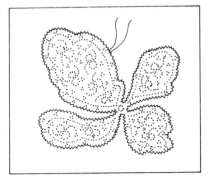

18   *Geometric quilting with additional motifs.*

19   *Lace appliqué using straight and zig-zag stitches.*

Lace appliqué
Zig-zag

Add a different texture by cutting motifs from Guipure lace and building up a spray of flowers. Press Bondaweb to wrong side of lace, peel off paper backing, cut out motifs and place in position on right side of satin. Press.

Use machine embroidery thread to match the lace and zig-zag stitch 1.5mm wide, 1mm long, and stitch round motif over the edge. Carefully trim off any loose pieces of lace. If using motifs with petals, attach by stitching a small, straight stitch from the centre between the petals in order to leave the flower loose. Add stems, outlines of leaves etc., by couching a topstitching thread or fine crochet cotton, using zig-zag stitch.

Gauging

Small areas of crisp fabrics can be decorated with parallel rows of large, straight stitching. Insert all the rows, fastening off by reversing at one side and leaving loose ends of equal length at the other. Take hold of the bobbin threads in pairs and pull up to ruche the fabric. Check the ends of all threads are still equal in length. Do not press the fabric. Cut to size and back with another piece of fabric or lining.

Curved edges

Where angled edges are to be folded under eg. corners of shaped pockets, curved yokes that are to be applied with an overlaid seam, insert a row of large straight stitches 1mm outside the seam line and ease up the thread a little until the curved edge curls over to the wrong side. Baste and press, then proceed in the usual way.

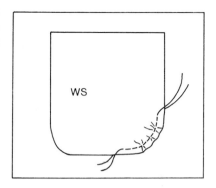

WS

20 *Easing a corner before folding under.*

Attaching elastic

Open-mesh elastic is easier to sew than conventional core elastic. Measure the elastic round the body and cut to size making sure it will go over the shoulders, hips etc. Join the ends, mark elastic in four. Divide the garment into four. Slide elastic over wrong side of garment, match the join to a seam and sew with zig-zag or overlock stitch. Stretch the elastic as you sew, matching up the marks. Attach narrow elastic with one row down the middle, wide elastic with a row down each edge.

Attaching Velcro

When using Spot-Ons, stitch the firmer hook section to the underside by stitching in a triangle across the circle. Use a small, straight or zig-zag stitch. Stitch the soft, upper circle by hand or with a small zig-zag or overlock stitch all round the outer edge.

Attach strip Velcro with a small zig-zag stitch round the outer edge. Where there will be movement in wear, eg. waist fastening, stitch across the under piece 5mm (1/4in.) within the edge at the end. This prevents creaking in wear.

Group Five: Crisp fancy-weave fabrics

Jacquard-weave taffeta, self-colour brocade, brocade with metallic yarn, moiré taffeta, cloqué, ribbed taffeta, ottoman.

With the exception of moiré taffeta, all these fabrics fray badly because of the loose or floating yarns that form the pattern. The raised bubbles that characterize cloqué are, in some cases, pressed into the fabric but in more expensive types a very fine, gauze, backing fabric made of loosely-woven threads, catches the top fabric in places to pull it into blisters. The yarns of both layers will fray badly.

Needle – 70-80. Regular; although if problems are encountered with brocade, especially those with metal, use 90 ballpoint.

Stitch – Straight: 2.5mm long. Zig-zag: 3mm wide, 1.5mm long. Straight stitch may be deflected by the design on the fabric.

Thread – Polyester. Place paper beneath if necessary.

Seams – Open: neaten raw edges flat with zig-zag. Raw edges of bias seams may stretch. If so, zig-zag over a thread which can be pulled up to reduce puckering. Puckered seam lines can be flattened by putting narrow strips of Wundaweb (or Wundatrim which is narrower) under the seam allowances and pressing, with the seam stretched out and pinned to the pressing surface. Edges of badly fraying brocade can be neatened with strips of soft net or veiling. Cut the strips 1.5cm (⅝in.) wide in any direction, fold in half down the middle, slide over the raw edge of the seam and attach with zig-zag 3mm (⅛in.) wide, 2 mm (¹⁄₁₆in.) long, sewing through all layers.

Hems and edges – Blind hem: with the exception of moire taffeta hems can be 3cm (1¼in.) or more deep and blind-hemmed. Do not fold under the raw edge; it should be neatened with zig-zag and left to lie flat. Wundaweb hems: brocade and some jacquards can have a 3cm (1¼in.) hem secured with Wundaweb. Wundaweb can also be used to control fraying on cut edges such as openings and it also helps to insert

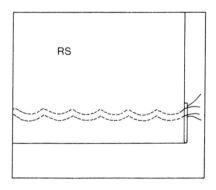

RS

21   *Twin needle hem on crisp fabric.*

small pieces in collar points etc. Twin needle hem: for use on moiré taffeta and ottoman particularly. Turn up hem once and baste, neaten raw edge. Baste hem to garment, pressing hard to make an imprint. With fabric right side up, work a row of twin needle beside the mark, using twin needle 2. Few fabrics with a woven pattern can be successfully decorated because the beauty is in the design. However drop feed free embroidery can look good on moiré taffeta. It should be worked with a hoop but it will not require backing. Plan a random design but mark the main points on the wrong side using fabric pen. Remove the foot, drop the feed, loosen the top tension and use straight stitch length 2mm. Work from wrong side of fabric. Variations can be achieved by using a twin needle, small space, by using contrasting colours or random coloured thread and by using a wide zig-zag stitch closed up to 1mm long to create solid lines. Tighten the bottom tension as necessary.

Blind hemming

Hems can be invisibly stitched on all except thin or transparent fabrics. The hem is easy to sew on straight edges, it requires more care if it is shaped, as the fullness has to be eased in as you stitch.

The blind hem stitch makes three straight stitches followed by one zig-zag. The finer the fabric, the narrower should be the zig-zag or it penetrates the fabric too far and the stitch shows on the right side.

Put blind hem foot on the machine. Turn up the hem and pin or baste below the hem edge. Prepare a test piece in the same way. Fold the hem back and put the fabric under the foot so that the straight stitch runs on the single hem edge and the zig-zag moves left and catches a thread of the fold, that is, the outer layer of fabric. Adjust the foot and the zig-zag until the result is perfect when you flatten the hem. Control the stitching carefully.

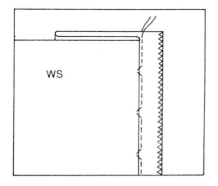

22 *Hem folded flat and blind-hem stitched.*

Interfacing: Sew-in interfacing can be attached with the blind hemmer, stitching on the interfacing and catching the garment with the

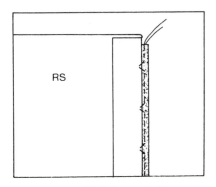

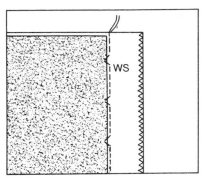

23 *Using blind-hem stitch to attach sew-in interfacing.*

24 *Sewing free edge of iron-on interfacing with blind-hem stitch.*

zig-zag. Also, where iron-on interfacing extends to the centre point, the edge can be secured flat with blind hemming. Make sure the stitching runs just to the inside of the garment. Thread colour must match fabric rather than the interfacing.

Rolled hem

It helps to give yourself a firm edge to roll especially if the hemline is curved, by inserting a row of straight machine stitching 2-3mm (⅛in.) outside the seam line. Before rolling the hem trim the raw edge to 1mm from the stitching.

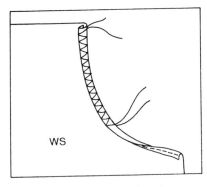

25 *Rolled hem secured with zig-zag stitch.*

Machine-stitched hem

If a hem is to be sewn by machine, there is little point in pressing it carefully to avoid an imprint. So use this fact to help. Press the turned-up hem along the edge to make an imprint that shows through on the right side of the garment. Stitch the hem, right side up, inside the imprint running the edge of the foot along the mark.

Neatening

Never reverse zig-zag stitch when neatening raw edges. It wastes thread, makes a lumpy edge and in most cases the seam will shortly be trimmed off anyway. If your machine has a tie-off facility use this at the end of rows of neatening.

Group Six: Soft semi-transparent fabrics

Cotton voile, polyester voile, Swiss cotton, French voile, Robia voile, Tergal sheer, muslin, ninon, georgette.

These fabrics are often plain or with small printed designs, some have a spaced-out woven design often in self-colour but in shiny yarn. Some of these fabrics also feature metallic yarns, often in stripes. All the fabrics fray, although cotton voile frays surprisingly little. Depending on the garment being made, a lining may be necessary.

Needle – 70-80 Universal. If the fabric is closely woven you may need to use a ballpoint needle.

Stitch – Straight: 2mm long. Zig-zag: 3mm wide, 1.5mm long.

Thread – Polyester or mercerized.

Seams – French seams: finished at 3-5mm (⅛-¼in.) width is suitable on all fabrics with the possible exception of firm cotton voile. On this fabric use narrow seams, finished with a line of zig-zag worked over both raw edges. Hairline seam: except on badly fraying fabrics this is suitable for full garments provided the seams will not be subjected to strain. Seams on the bias can be stitched once with a very small zig-zag stitch, others may need a row of straight stitching finished with zig-zag over the top. In both cases, trim off surplus fabric.

Hems and edges – Narrow hem: all fabrics can be turned in twice and stitched; most fabrics will require basting first. With especially springy or fraying fabrics, use a small zig-zag stitch to hold the hem. Alternatively, use a decorative stitch such as the running zig-zag, set at full width. This could feature matching or contrasting thread. Twin needle hem: turn up and baste a deep hem, folding in the raw edge to control the fraying. Use a twin needle, two contrasting threads, a simple decorative stitch and stitch the hem right side up, following the shadow created by the hem.

The plain or shell hemming foot can be used on most of the fabrics in this group. Cut the edge cleanly to remove frays, stitch at once.

Avoid facings, if possible, unless the garment has been backed with lining. Collarless necklines can be finished with binding.

Self fabric appliqué

When using patterned voile, small areas such as yokes and cuffs, and accessories such as bags can have additional decoration using the same fabric. If the fabric is plain, you might consider using lace or a quite different fabric. The motif on the fabric should be fairly dense and woven or flocked on the background rather than printed. Simple solid outlines such as leaves are most suitable. Cut out the garment fabric.

Press the spare or second fabric to Bondaweb. Peel off the paper backing and cut out the motifs. Arrange the motifs carefully, filling the spaces between the existing ones. If the base fabric is plain, arrange the motifs in diagonal lines, facing various directions, to obtain a random effect. Press all motifs in position. Using a perfectly matching machine embroidery thread and a small, close zig-zag, stitch round the motifs. On completion, press on the wrong side.

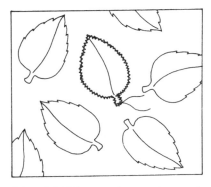

26 *Self fabric appliqué using semi-transparent fabric.*

27 *Shadow patterns using semi-transparent fabric.*

Quick shadow patterns
Straight stitch

A pretty decoration for semi-transparent fabrics, this must be the quickest and easiest of all decorative features. Plan a band or border about 5cm (2in.) wide and mark out a figure-of-eight outline on the right side of the fabric. Turn fabric wrong side up and place leaf-shaped pieces of coloured fabric, trimmed with pinking shears, inside the outline. Use woven fabric that will wash the same way as the garment and make sure colours will not run. Place a second piece of the garment fabric wrong side down on top and baste together outside the design. This second layer might well be the hem edge or facing folded back, or it can be a separate piece of fabric. With right side up, stitch along the marked outline to enclose the contrast shapes.

Textured loops
Drop feed; zig-zag

Suitable for fine semi-transparent fabrics, this decoration is equally interesting on both sides so experiment before working on a garment. The design is stitched in small circles which appear as little bulges on the upper side and textured loops on the under side. Use a strongly contrasting colour thread. Put the fabric in a hoop and secure tightly.

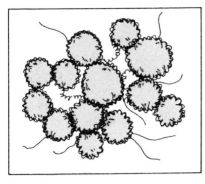

28 *Textured loops with contrast fabric beneath a soft semi-transparent fabric.*

Loosen the upper tension and tighten the bottom tension. Work quickly in circles, starting the next one immediately, so that they touch, until you have an irregular shape.

A variation of this involves putting a piece of soft fabric underneath, in a contrasting colour, tightening the upper tension and loosening the lower tension a little. Stitch circles and trim away surplus contrasting fabric. This produces a harder, flatter motif.

Simplified Textured Appliqué

Straight and zig-zag stitch. Although any scraps can be used for appliqué, if it is your first attempt at it, you will find the following tips helpful.

Use fabrics that will wash in the same way as the garment. Do not use contrasting colours, choose the same colour or various subtle tones of the background fabric. Work on firm background fabrics, not silky or fine ones. Avoid the plain or shiny appliqué fabrics. It is much easier to use textures such as loop or bouclé, fine towelling velour, suede fabric, so that the fabric itself creates the design and you can keep your stitching to a minimum. Choose a thread to match or tone with the fabrics, not a contrast which would make every stitch obvious. Choose a design with a simple curved outline avoiding sharp corners. If you choose flowers, draw a stylised outline for simplicity, not separate petals which have to overlap and add bulk as well as additional raw edges to be covered. Finally, plan a design that you can add to if all goes well. For example, try a single flower on a stem for the right half of a jacket. Add leaves if you wish. If that was successful, work a second flower slightly differently on the left side – never try to make them match, it is too difficult. The same motif could then be adapted for a collar, hat or bag if you wish. Try to decorate small areas only that can be disposed of if things go wrong. Always do the decoration before finally cutting the fabric to size.

There are two main methods of working appliqué. With the first, back the appliqué fabric with Bondaweb to keep it smooth and control fraying. Peel off the paper backing. Mark the motif with fabric pen, chalk pencil or a line of straight stitching and cut out. Place in position on backing fabric and press until it adheres. Using a wide, close zig-zag, stitch round the outer edge. If possible, reduce the width at points and angles. When turning corners, stop with the needle down on the outside of the angle, lift the foot, turn the fabric, lower the foot and continue. The needle then comes down on the inside of the angle for the next stitch. You may need to loosen the top tension a little for a good, smooth stitch. The edges of appliqué can be emphasised by zig-zag over a fine cord or topstitching thread. If the appliqué fabric is thick, sew round first with a small, open zig-zag, then stitch a second time with a wider, closer stitch.

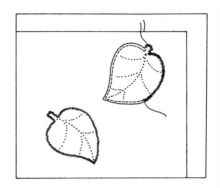

29 *Textured appliqué.*

Pull all ends of thread to the wrong side to fasten off.

The second method involves stitching from the wrong side. Draw the design required on the wrong side of the base fabric. On the right side, baste a piece of the appliqué fabric wrong side down over the whole area. Using a straight stitch and with fabric wrong side up stitch round the outline. On the right side trim the appliqué fabric away close to the stitching. With wrong side up and a wide close zig-zag stitch with slightly tightened top tension, stitch over the line of straight stitching to finish.

Various stitches and patterns can be added from the right side as required.

Group Seven: Fine, soft, woven fabrics

Silk crêpe de chine, silk twill, silk Habutai, silk foulard, silk satin, Jap silk, Bemberg, silk jacquard, polyester crêpe de chine, polyester, jacquard, viscose jacquard, damask weave silk, printed crêpe, printed polyester, crinkle-finish polyester, polyester crêpon, polyester satin, pongee, Tricel.

Colours and designs in all these fabrics are usually fairly sophisticated; most of them are expensive and would be used for dresses and blouses. Most of them, even the plain fabrics look best without much stitched decoration. The synthetic fabrics and the twill weaves may fray, but otherwise, it is not a problem when handling fabrics such as crêpe de chine. Gathers will often be featured. On some plain fabrics in this group, it is best to use sew-in interfacing. Test such products as Fold-a-Band before putting them in a garment in case the adhesive affects the smooth surface.

Needle – 70. Universal gives the best results. Place fabric on paper if stitching puckers. If bias stitching is uneven, use a 70 Universal needle instead.

Stitch – Straight: 2mm long. Zig-zag: 2.5mm wide, 1.5mm long.

Thread – Polyester.

Seams – French: finished at 5mm (¼in.) width or more on polyester fabrics which tend to be bulkier than silk. Open seams: these should be used on dresses, neatening the raw edges with zig-zag. If the fabric frays and it is thin, the edge may be turned under and zig-zagged over the fold with a small stitch; length 2mm, width 2.5mm. Bias edges will stretch under this treatment but they will press flat with care.

Hems and edges – Narrow hem: either use the hemming foot or trim and baste a narrow hem to be finished with a small, straight stitch. Deep hem: on skirts and dresses the hem should be made 2-7cm (¾in.-2¾in.) deep depending on how shaped it is. Turn and baste the hem and press the fold. Neaten the raw edge with small zig-zag. If the hem is fairly straight, fold under the raw edge to give a firmer base on which to zig-zag. Finish with blind hemstitch or by hand on thin fabrics. Edges can be faced or bound to finish.

Ribbon stripes

Narrow satin ribbon 3mm (⅛in.) wide makes an attractive decoration on soft, lightweight fabrics. The ribbon can be used as a contrast, applied to look like stripes on plain fabric on a yoke or round cuffs, or carefully placed to add more stripes to striped fabric. Choose the colour of the ribbon carefully so that it blends into the design of the garment. For best results, apply it only to interfaced areas of the garment and in straight lines.

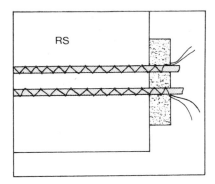

30 *Attaching narrow ribbon using wide zig-zag.*

Attach soft iron-on Vilene to the wrong side of the fabric. Do not cut the section to size as the ribbon will reduce it slightly, but do mark the outline. If the fabric has no guiding line such as stripes, make a row of dots using fabric pen where one edge of the ribbon will fall. Use thread that is a perfect match for the ribbon and set the stitch to zig-zag 4mm (just over ⅛in.) wide and 3mm (⅛in.) long. On most fabrics you will be able to place the ribbon in position on the right side of the fabric and simply zig-zag over it, taking care not to pull the ribbon. Use dual feed if you have it. If the fabric is slippery or if you found the test piece difficult to do, attach the ribbon to the fabric with basting tape before stitching.

A lattice design is an alternative to stripes but the fabric may pucker unless Stitch-n-Tear is used underneath in addition to Vilene.

Seam imprints

Take especial care with all fabrics, especially those that are soft or plain colour, to see that seams do not leave an imprint when pressed. After pressing the line of stitches, use the toe of the iron on the seam rather than the whole sole. Always press twice lightly rather than once heavily.

If you do make an imprint, run the iron over it immediately, while still warm, on the wrong side of the fabric, underneath the bulk of the seam. Careful use of a lightly wrung out damp muslin pressing cloth may help on fabrics that are not silk.

Scallops
Automatic stitch

Suitable for soft closely woven fabrics, scallops can be added to a finished edge on sleeves, collars, cuffs. They can also be added to each edge of a shirt band fastening. Cord the scallops with fine crochet cotton or embroidery thread. Have lightweight Vilene between the layers of fabric. This might be Stitch-n-Tear if it is a strap opening or

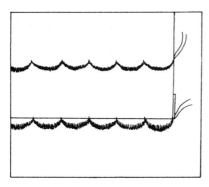

31 *Showing corded scallops on fabric but standing free and, below, used as an edging.*

cuff. Attach cording foot with hole for cord, or satin stitch foot. Place fabric under foot with fold against the needle, place cord in position under foot and select the stitch. Place paper or Stitch-n-Tear under the whole area, not just beneath the fabric. Work the scallops guiding the fabric so that the needle catches the edge with the three stitches at the far left. The cord will follow the scallop automatically even if you haven't a foot with a hole in it. Gently ease away the paper on completion.

A mock band or strap can be formed by folding the fabric again 2-3cm (3/4-1 1/4 in.) from the first line, stitch the scallops then open out the fabric again. To make it more defined add a row of straight stitch 3-5mm (1/4-1/8 in.) from the scallops before opening the fabric.

Quick spot-marking
To mark the position for attaching a button, beginning a line of stitching or placement spot for starting a piece of braid etc., note that many plain, smooth fabrics can be adequately marked by making a cross with your finger nail. The mark will remain for several minutes.

Satin stitch edge
This is useful for sashes, scarves, waterfall collars etc. Using a small zig-zag, stitch over a fine cord or topstitching thread, on the seam line, within the raw edge. Trim the fabric close to the stitching, place on Stitch-n-Tear and stitch again, this time with a wide, close zig-zag.

Controlling fraying or fly-away ends of synthetic thread
When stitching raw edges for neatening etc., odd rogue fraying yarns can be controlled by licking your finger tips and smoothing them back into place just before you stitch over them. Similarly, if after a lot of stitching the ends of the thread twist and snarl, run moist fingers along them before beginning the next line of stitching.

Shirring

Use elastic thread that has plenty of stretch. Beware of those with less elastic and more thread because they have insufficient strength to pull up the fabric.

Wind the elastic on to the bobbin. Do this on the machine as if it were ordinary thread. (If you can only wind the bobbins via the needle you cannot do this.) The elastic must be tight on the bobbin. Thread the machine using ordinary thread on top. Use 3mm (⅛in.) straight stitch or any other utility stitches. Work the first row of stitching, fabric right side up, and subsequent rows parallel with it. Use the foot as a space guide and smooth out the fabric. If possible, sew garment seams first and stitch round and round to avoid too many ends that can pull out easily. Work as many rows as necessary to reduce the fabric as you want. On completion, tie off the thread ends on the wrong side and also stitch across them to secure. Hold the shirring in the steam from boiling water which will release the tension on the elastic and wrinkle the fabric more. You may have to loosen the tension on the bobbin. Use the spare case if you have one.

An alternative method is to zig-zag over two lengths of elastic, pulling as you sew. Make sure the zig-zag does not catch the elastic.

Stitching parallel with an edge

There are several ways of keeping straight. If the line is to be close to the edge, use the outside or inside edge of the foot, running it along the edge of the fabric. Alternatively, use the central groove and move the needle to the left. A wider spacing is obtained by using the edge of the foot and having the needle on the left. For a much wider space make use of the grooves marked on the machine base to the right of the needle or, if that is insufficient, stick a piece of basting tape across the bed, parallel with the outer groove. When stitching, watch the edge of the fabric and the marker, not the needle movement. If you feel you must have marks on the fabric, set your adjustable marker to the correct distance and make a row of dots using a fabric pen. (Use the one that makes marks that disappear automatically to avoid having to wash the fabric.)

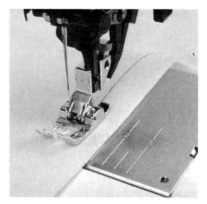

32   *Using grooves on needle plate for a straight line of stitching.*

Group Eight: Thin, soft woven fabrics

Lining, fabrics including taffeta, Synabel, Bemberg, acetate, satin, twill.

All these fabrics fray and after some wear will suffer slippage of yarns at the seams. Some satin lining is so loosely woven, slippage or movement of yarns will occur as the seams are stitched. If linings hang loose and are not stitched to the garment all round, raw edges must be neatened for at least the bottom half of all seams, otherwise long fraying yarns will soon be hanging below the hemline.

Needle – 70. Regular. If stitch deflection occurs or machine misses stitches on polyester, use Universal needle.

Stitch – Straight: 2mm long. Zig-zag: 2.5mm wide, 1.5mm long.

Thread – Polyester.

Seams – Narrow: straight stitch 5mm (¼in.) inside raw edge, zig-zag over raw edges. Press seam to one side. Although fraying will continue for a while, it will soon stop if you trim off the longer yarns. Open seams: although you may sometimes want to use open seams in lining, they are not easy to do. After stitching it requires care to press open the seam allowances. Raw edges should be zig-zagged but they will stretch. Pressing the seam flat again will invariably produce imprints on the fabric. If the lining is in a full garment, the raw edges can be turned under before zig-zagging but it makes a bulky seam if it is a fitted garment.

Hems and edges – Narrow: fold over twice, press and stitch or use hemming foot. Alternatively turn the hem on to the right side, making it 1.5-3cm (⅝-1¼in.) deep and stitch decoratively, perhaps in a contrasting colour or even metallic thread, or with a twin needle. Lace edging: trim the lining and zig-zag the raw edge. Place lace edging on the right side overlapping by 5mm (¼in.) or almost the width of the lace to prevent it pulling away. Attach with zig-zag or small decorative stitch worked along the upper edge of the lace. This hem finish can be used on underlayers of full skirts that have something such as organza over the top. If the fabric does not fray badly, omit the zig-zagging along the edge, attach the lace, then trim off the excess fabric close to the stitching. Facings: neck edges etc., can be faced but it adds bulk. A better finish is to roll a narrow hem and secure with a small zig-zag stitch worked to enclose the hem completely.

Eyelets

Eyelets are a utility feature for buckles with prongs, for lacing ribbons and other fastenings; they can also be used decoratively on parts of garments, as borders or to embellish fabric already decorated. Modern machines have automatic stitches that make pretty eyelets resembling flowers; computerized machines have an eyelet facility at the touch of a button.

However, most machines including basic zig-zag models have a pronged eyelet plate available which is fitted over the feed teeth. Thread the machine, drop the teeth, attach the plate and set the stitch to medium zig-zag or automatic pattern. If fabric is loosely woven, force it over the prong in the plate. For large holes snip the fabric or punch a hole. Some automatic eyelets are intended to be cut out afterwards. If you use an automatic pattern, use one that throws stitches to the right and therefore reinforces the middle of the hole. Stitch round the hole, feeding the fabric in a clockwise direction. Stitch round once quickly to seal the edge, the second time to neaten and reinforce. With big holes, sew round a third time. Finish with a couple of straight stitches to fasten off.

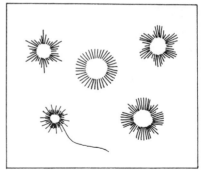

33 *Eyelets using a variety of stitches.*

Feathery stitching

Zig-zag stitch. This stitch is worked with the fabric in a hoop but without dropping the feed. It is best worked on a firm fabric such as cotton so that no support is needed. Use a stitch 3mm (⅛in.) wide and 2-3mm (⅛in.) long and move the hoop from side to side as you sew, rather like driving a car and turning the steering wheel evenly from side to side. If you use check fabric, you can make a border, using the checks as a steering guide.

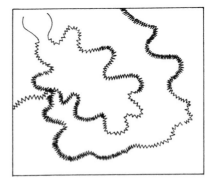

34 *Feathery stitching.*

Group Nine: Lightweight, crisp wovens

Silk and polyester taffeta, paper taffeta, slub polyester, fine slub silk, shantung, raw silk.

These fabrics are closely woven from slippery yarns and they fray badly.

Needle – 80 Regular. If stitch deflection occurs, 70 Universal.

Stitch – Straight: 1.5mm long. Zig-zag: 3mm wide, 1.5mm long.

Thread – Polyester and mercerized.

Seams – French: finished at 5mm (¼in.) width in finer fabrics. Open: to be used on thicker fabrics and garments such as dresses. Neaten raw edges with zig-zag. Welt: a flat seam that looks attractive on silk shirts etc., stitch with wrong sides together, trim one raw edge to 3mm (⅛in.) and press. Fold under the wider raw edge, baste flat and stitch again parallel with first row. Any stitching on yoke, cuffs or collar should match.

Hems and edges – Narrow hem: use this except where a deep hem is required on dresses. The hemming foot can be used on all these fabrics although it is difficult to keep the hem even as the foot passes over French seams. Blind hem: finish medium and deep hems with zig-zag and then secure with blind hemstitch. Wundaweb: hems on skirts, frills etc., can be trimmed to 3mm (⅛in.) zig-zagged along the raw edge, then held in place with Wundaweb. Test on a scrap of fabric to make sure it does not show. Zig-zag hem: edges of frills can be stitched with small zig-zag over a folded edge. Trim away excess fabric on the wrong side. On some fabrics a picot edge can be made by zig-zagging over the raw edge with the needle just catching the fabric when it moves to the left. Facings: necklines etc., can be faced if required. Attach interfacing to the garment, testing iron-on types first as they may be visible on plain fabric.

Hems using hemming foot

Where possible, stitch the hem before joining seams that run into the hem or even turn the hem before cutting to size. Trim the raw edge cleanly leaving 5-6mm (¼in.) turn-up. Attach the straight stitch or the shell edge foot and stitch a hem on a scrap of fabric, adjusting the stitch and practising holding the fabric. Use your right hand to hold the raw edge vertically over the curled toe of the foot. You will also have to hold it slightly to the left in front of the foot. Hold the fabric fairly taut. Take care in adjusting the stitch to match that on the remainder of the garment. A stitch on the same setting will usually be a little smaller when hemming feet are used.

Stitch the garment hem immediately while you still remember how to hold the fabric. Fold over the hem at the start, put it under the foot and stitch for about 1cm (⅜in.) then stop, lift the foot, and lift the raw edge, wrapping it over the front of the foot. Lower the foot and stitch the entire hem. This technique ensures that the hem is stitched from the beginning; there is no need to do it when practising or when stitching frills and other items that can be trimmed afterwards.

You will probably not be able to use the hemming foot on bias edges although it can be used on curves and circles.

Crushed tucks
Straight stitch

A crunchy decoration for small areas such as yokes, panels or bags, this works best on light to medium crisp synthetic fabrics that are springy and do not flatten easily. It is very quick to do on a fabric with printed or woven stripes. Folding the fabric wrong sides together make a series of tucks the width of the foot. Do not press. Now work rows of stitching at right angles, across the tucks first in one direction to flatten them then in the other to flatten them the opposite way. Make the rows 2cm (¾in.) apart. Cut out to size.

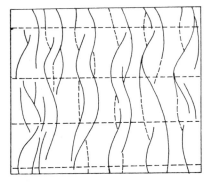

35   *Crushed tucks in soft fabric that does not crease.*

Gathering threads
On dark fabrics, change the bobbin to one that is wound with a lighter colour. When you pull up the gathers, the stitching will be easier to find.

Marking buttonholes
Mark buttonhole positions with fabric pen, extending lines so that the ends are visible beside the buttonhole foot and they don't get hidden by it.

Darts
Before stitching pairs of matching darts, measure along the fold of each from the seam line and chalk a line across the dart point at right angles as a clear sign where to end the stitching.

Group Ten: Lightweight matt woven fabrics

Swiss cotton, broderie anglaise, cotton mousseline, cotton/modal fabrics, cotton crêpon, leno-weave cotton, madras cotton.

The fabrics in this group are easy to sew. They may fray a little but should not be troublesome.

Needle – 80 Regular.

Stitch – Straight: 1.5mm long. Zig-zag: 3mm wide, 1.5mm long.

Thread – Mercerized and polyester.

Seams – French seams: finished at 5mm (¼in.) width on fine fabrics. Open seams: edges can be neatened with zig-zag or folded under and edge stitched.

Hems and edges – Narrow hem: hems folded and stitched 5mm-1cm (¼-⅜in.) wide are suitable. The hemming foot can be used but not on striped or check fabric unless you have dual feed to help get the pattern matched. Zig-zag edge: depending on the garment, the edge may be folded under, pressed and zig-zagged over the fold with a small stitch. Trim off the excess fabric on the wrong side. Necklines, armholes etc. can be faced or bound.

Scalloped double edge

This is a very attractive edging for collars etc., in light and medium weight fabrics. If pre-decorated fabric such as broderie anglaise is used, this edging echoes the design.

Cut collar pieces and attach iron-on Vilene to the under layer. Press Bondaweb to one layer, place both together right sides out and press. Try this first on a scrap of fabric and if it makes the collar too stiff put a narrow strip of Bondaweb around the outer edge only. Replace the paper pattern and mark the outer seam line using fabric pen. Attach the embroidery foot, set the machine to scallop stitch, loosening the top

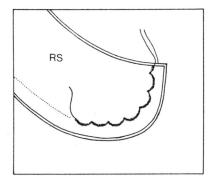

36   *Scallops to form outer edge.*

RS

63

tension slightly or tightening the bottom. With collar right side up, stitch on the marked line. The collar is probably firm enough not to need Stitch-n-Tear underneath unless you are sewing on fine voile or other soft lightweight fabric.

Finish by carefully trimming off the surplus fabric close to the stitching, using the points of small scissors.

Ribbon slots

Using firm fabric such as cotton, make a line of vertical buttonholes, in pairs, for threading ribbon. The ribbon can be drawn up, or left flat. For an attractive effect use contrasting colour ribbon and make the buttonholes at least 3mm (⅛in.) shorter than the width of the ribbon.

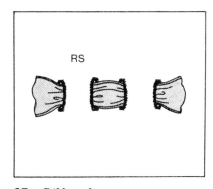
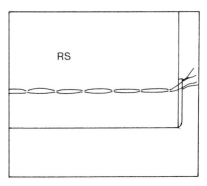

37   *Ribbon slots.*   38   *Double thread topstitching.*

Double thread topstitching
Straight or zig-zag stitch

This can be very effective on a number of fabrics. Using two reels of thread, matching or contrasting with the fabric, even two different colours together, an interesting topstitch can be added to edges, hems, cuffs, pockets etc. Insert a bobbin wound with thread to match the garment, put the two reels of thread on the top of the machine using both reel holders. If your machine does not have a second holder, wind two bobbins and use them one on top of each other. Thread each separately through the machine making sure they pass one each side of the tension disc, then thread both through the eye of a size 100 needle. Use a 3mm (⅛in.) straight stitch and stitch the design required.

Triple needle stitching

Various stitches. This needle is seldom used, yet it makes the most attractive patterns very easily. Bands of coloured stitching can be added to sleeves, hems etc., or a window-pane check design can be made over an entire area. Except where a few lines only are to be used, work the stitching before cutting the garment to shape. Use three different coloured threads, or shaded threads or use one colour in the central eye and another in the two outer eyes. Soft fabrics should be double or have Vilene or Stitch-n-Tear beneath them. Try out various stitches including straight and zig-zag remembering that total width of all three lines cannot exceed the maximum zig-zag width.

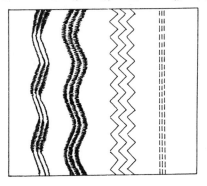

39   *Various stitches using triple needle.*

Seam ends

If you find your seams wrinkle when you start stitching, particularly on fine fabrics, place a small, folded piece of fabric under the foot, start machining and continue on to the garment.

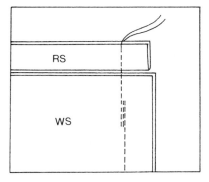

Knots

After sitting down at the machine but before beginning to sew, snip off the knots of your lines of basting to prevent them becoming trampled by the stitching.

40   *Begin stitching on spare fabric for smooth seam.*

Group Eleven:
Closely-woven lightweight fabrics

Cotton lawn, polyester/cotton, Tana lawn, light poplin, fine cotton twill, percale, cambric, mercerized cotton.

These fabrics are easy to handle and fray very little. Bias stitching does not present problems.

Needle – 80 Regular.

Stitch – Straight: 2mm long. Zig-zag: 3mm wide, 1.5mm long.

Thread – Mercerized or polyester.

Seams – French: for loose garments such as nightwear and blouses. Open: neaten edges with zig-zag or fold under the edge and finish with straight stitch or zig-zag. Narrow: provided there will not be any strain in wear, seams on loose garments can be stitched with an overlock or overedge stitch set to 2mm (¹⁄₁₆in.) length, 4mm (just over ⅛in.) width.

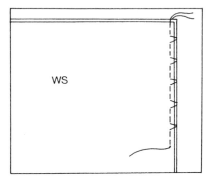

41 *Stitch a narrow seam using one row of overlock or overedge stitch.*

Hems and edges – Binding: narrow binding finished at 3-5mm (⅛-¼in.) is suitable. Narrow hem: fabric can be folded twice and stitched with an open decorative stitch, possibly in contrasting thread. Hems can also be turned using hemming foot. Deep hems: stitch with blind hemming. Alternatively use twin needle or decorative stitch but avoid close satin stitches as the hem would be hardened.

Circular hem

Lightweight fabrics make attractive circular skirts. Hems must be kept to minimum depth. Allow skirt to hang for a couple of days to give time for the weave to open up and stretch, where it falls on the bias. Mark the hem level and cut off, leaving 1cm (⅜in.) for the hem. Fold the hem edge twice narrowly, hold it taut and stitch with a medium width zig-zag or overedge stitch. Alternatively trim the skirt leaving 3mm (⅛in.) hem. Zig-zag the raw edge then fold it under 3mm (⅛in.) and straight stitch

1-2mm inside the fold. Stitch with right side up so that the edge is held flat by the machine bed.

Ribbon 3-5mm ($\frac{1}{8}$-$\frac{1}{4}$in.) wide can also be added to give the skirt extra swing. To do this, either zig-zag the edge, then apply the ribbon on top, allowing it to extend beyond the skirt; use a small decorative stitch to attach; or roll and baste a double hem, then attach the ribbon slightly above the edge, attaching it with skirt right side up.

Edgestitcher

If you have an old straight stitch machine this is one of the pieces of equipment you will find in the accessory box. It is a flat piece of metal with a number of slots, a sliding part, and a needle hole. The front curls up slightly. The central slot in front of the needle slot can be used as a feed for ribbon and braid; the needle will stitch it along the middle. Use for edge stitching, tucks, attaching lace. It requires practice to use this tool accurately.

Set the machine to a straight stitch. To do edge stitching fold the fabric and feed it through one of the left-hand slots. To attach lace, feed fabric through a left slot and the lace in the right-hand slot.

Ribbon patterns

Ribbons of any width or design are a quick form of decoration. Plain ribbon 5mm ($\frac{1}{4}$in.) or more wide can be attached with a small zig-zag stitch worked over the edge or a straight stitch worked inside the bead edge of the ribbon. A line of open or satin stitch embroidery pattern can be worked down the middle. Fancy patterns can also be used along the edge to hold the ribbon in place; interesting effects can be created by using a perfectly matching thread and a stitch set to a suitable length and width so that it forms an extension of the ribbon and looks like part of it. Patterns that need matching on both edges are difficult and have to be controlled. Try and stitch in the same direction along each side to avoid puckering. Use dual feed if you have it. Single satin ribbon will slip less than one which is satin on both sides. Make sure you have a guide line along which to run one edge of the ribbon eg. fold, hemline, row of basting or chalk marks or fabric pen dots. Wide ribbons can be fixed in place first if necessary with basting tape or Wundatrim, although, of course, Wundatrim is also a way of attaching ribbons permanently.

Ribbon that is 3mm ($\frac{1}{8}$in.) wide can be attached as described on page 56. Alternatively a very effective method of adding stripes is to use a twin needle which make a double row of stitching, one inside each edge.

Jacquard or printed ribbon is decorative in itself and looks best attached with a straight stitch worked just inside the bead in a thread to

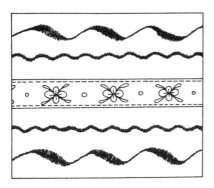

42 *Combining jacquard ribbon and automatic embroidery.*

match that area of the ribbon. However, further stitching can be effective using the colours of the ribbon and spaced on each side. You may have an automatic pattern that echoes the ribbon design.

Joining braid or ribbon

If possible, attach while garment is flat, as soon as the nearest guiding seam is stitched. Small pieces of fabric are easier to turn. For example, to add ribbon to a yoke, cut out and attach Vilene to wrong side, attach ribbon parallel with seam lines and then join yoke to other sections, stitching parallel with ribbon.

To attach ribbon all round a skirt hem, join all seams, mark position of ribbon and unpick a small amount of one seam at that level. Attach ribbon, tuck ends into seam, restitch seam.

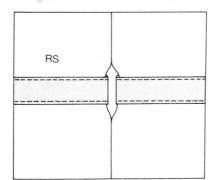

43 *Joining braid by inserting ends into seam.*

Mitres

Mark the point of the corner on the fabric. Attach the ribbon along the outside edge. On reaching the corner stop, turn and stitch across the ribbon at right angles and along the other edge. Return to the corner, fold the ribbon in the new direction and press. Complete the stitching.

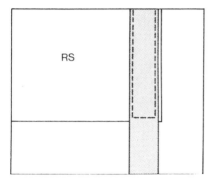

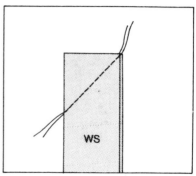

44 *Mitring ribbon at the corner while attaching it to an edge.*

45 *Stitching the mitre before attaching the ribbon.*

If you have to make the mitre before attaching the ribbon eg. in order to match a pattern, fold it right sides together and stitch across at 45 degrees. Cut off surplus and press. Place the mitre in position on the garment and begin stitching at that point.

Bold topstitching

If possible, stitch through an even number of layers throughout or the stitch will alter. Support the fabric with Vilene between the layers. Use a size 100 or 110 needle and a 3-4mm (⅛in.) stitch. Use normal thread in the bobbin. Loosen the top tension slightly and stitch from the right side. Use the foot to guide it parallel with an edge. If there is no edge close enough, make dots with a fabric pen or attach the edge guide to the quilting foot. A further alternative is to place a magnetic seam guide in position on the bed of the machine. If the thread you wish to use is not satisfactory on the top, wind it on the bobbin, loosen the bottom tension and stitch with the fabric wrong side up. Draw all threads to the underside to fasten off.

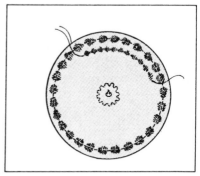

46 *Circular stitching: fabric right side up on point of drawing pin.*

Group Twelve:
Medium-weight, soft woven fabrics

Viyella, brushed cotton, Liberty Jubilee, wool gauze, wool mousseline, Clydella, light wool crêpe, wool challis, heavy cotton jacquard, embroidered cotton, viscose twill, brushed viscose, lightweight brushed acrylic, varuna wool.

The fabrics in this group are all easy to handle but they will fray, especially twill weaves. Bias stitching will stretch the fabric but it easily presses flat again.

Needle – 90 Regular.

Stitch – Straight: 2.5mm long. Zig-zag: 3.5mm wide, 1.5mm long.

Thread – Polyester, mercerized or corespun.

Seams – French: on children's clothes, blouses and nightwear. Open: neaten edges with zig-zag. The fraying will cease after a while. Welt: use if suitable for the garment.

Hems and edges – Narrow hem: roll a double hem and straight stitch or use an overedge or blindstitch to produce a shell edge. Deep hem: use blind hemstitch or, if suitable, straight stitch, possibly in contrast colour. Facings: all fabrics can be faced although wool dresses may be made less bulky by using lining for facings.

Zig-zag blocks

A method of making a simple line of decoration. It can be done on any basic zig-zag machine with 3 needle positions, namely left, centre and right. If worked on firm, closely-woven fabric such as cotton, no fabric backing will be required. Zig-zag blocks look particularly effective when worked in thread to match the fabric.

Set machine to a close narrow zig-zag, that is, one third of the total width the machine will do. This will be about 2mm (1/16in.). Practise to

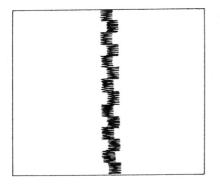

47   *Zig-zag blocks.*

see how many stitches will form a square block. Stitch the required number of stitches, starting with needle on the left; stop with needle up, move it to centre, stitch again; stop and move needle to right; stitch again. This makes 3 blocks. Work the next set moving the needle back to the left position and so on. Make sure needle is up when changing position.

Twin needle borders
Various stitches

The delights of using a twin needle are endless as an enormous variety of effects can be created.

Thread may match or contrast with the fabric. Threads of different colours can be used to produce a shaded effect. Random-dyed thread is also interesting to use.

A line of straight stitch twin needling will produce a flat double line or a raised tuck depending on the type of fabric and the size of the needle. Tightening the bottom tension will emphasise the tuck even more.

Any of the built-in embroidery stitches will produce interesting effects, especially making two lines in two colours. The stitch may be satin stitch or a close zig-zag. Metal thread can also be used. It is such a simple form of decoration that it is worth spending time working out an effective pattern.

Remember that the fabric is reduced by stitching so do not cut to size until stitching is complete. Where the border holds down a hem, try to leave another edge unfinished eg. shoulder seams, from which to adjust the length.

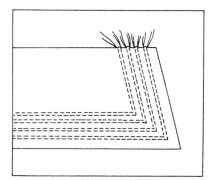

48 *Parallel rows of twin needle stitching produce raised tucks on soft medium-weight fabrics.*

Group Thirteen: Firm, crisp, woven fabrics

Medium weight plain and printed cotton, polyester/cotton, cotton twill, poplin, sailcloth, silk shantung, polyester shantung, Indian silk, slub silk, Liberty Country cotton, gingham.

None of the fabrics in this group are difficult to handle although those made from slippery yarns will fray. Most cottons have a finish applied in the final stages which tends to reduce the fraying.

Needle – 90 Regular.

Stitch – Straight: 2mm long. Zig-zag: 3mm wide, 1.5mm long.

Thread – Mercerized, polyester or corespun.

Seams – Open: neaten raw edges with zig-zag. Welt: suitable for all except possibly the silk fabrics. Narrow: either straight stitch then zig-zag over the edges, or if there will be little strain, stitch once only with an overlock or overedge stitch.

Hems and edges – Narrow or wide stitched hems: the raw edge can be zig-zagged and then stitched flat to secure, or on some fabrics the raw edge can be folded under. With printed cottons, spots, checks etc., sew hems with an open decorative stitch matching the thread colour with the print. Facings: suitable for all fabrics. Iron-on Vilene can be used on the garment.

Temporary hemline tucks
Stitch straight

On children's clothes which will have to be let down, turn up and stitch a normal depth hem 2-3cm (¾-1¼in.) deep. Above the hem fold, press and stitch two or three wide tucks. They can be from 5mm-2cm (¼-¾in.) deep and with 1-4cm (⅜-1½in.) between them depending on how much extra length has been allowed. Machine with a long,

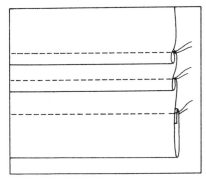 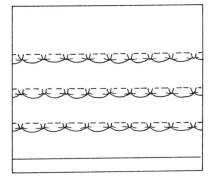

49 *Using a long stitch on tucks on children's clothes.*   **50** *Wide zig-zag or decorative stitch forms shell tucks.*

straight stitch, almost at maximum length. When the garment needs letting down, simply pull out the thread.

If you have insufficient extra fabric for wide tucks, stitch along the fold of each tuck with a full width zig-zag or open decorative stitch.

Simple piping
Straight stitch

This is a quick and easy way of emphasising style seams such as yokes, cuffs, collar edges using the same or contrast fabric. Advantages of it are that the seams are made firmer and it is useful as a decorative insertion round the edge of a coat or jacket that is lined to the edge as it will prevent the lining from bulging out and showing.

Cut bias strips of fabric barely 2cm (3/4in.) wide, fold wrong side inside and press. Place on right side of one piece of fabric with the centre of the strip on the seam line and the fold facing towards the garment. Stitch along the middle of the bias strip. Place second piece of fabric on top, right side down. Baste together if you prefer but most fabrics except slippery ones will grip quite well without it. Turn the assembly over and stitch again a fraction beside the first row of machining. When opened out and pressed there will be a neat 4mm (just over 1/8in.) bias fold in evidence.

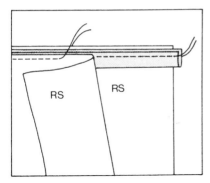

51 *Simple piping in a seam.*

Seeding
Straight stitch. Drop feed.

A novel decoration for covering whole areas eg. yoke, collar. Use matt, non-slippery fabric. Work on a big piece of fabric, before cutting to shape, put fabric in hoop, loosen the bottom tension and stitch in a random, doodling design. Do not allow lines to cross. On completion press iron-on Vilene to the wrong side then carefully withdraw the top thread which leaves a mass of tiny loops. Random-dyed thread creates an interesting effect. Use white thread on top for easy withdrawal.

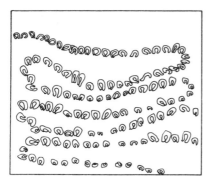

52 *Seeding – loops of thread form a random pattern.*

Alternative methods include zig-zag stitch, leaving in the top thread and also using topstitching thread on the bobbin and stitching from the wrong side.

Stitching along a fold
Crisp fabrics of all weights can be creased to form a flat fold on which to edge-stitch. Sit at the machine, grasp each end of the raw edge, or 20-30cm (8-12in.) of it if it is long, fold under 5-6mm (¼in.), hold the fabric very taut and run it over the edge of the machine bed or the table edge. Still holding it taut, place fabric under needle and begin edge-stitching.

Narrow seams
If you are going to use narrow or overlocked seams, reduce the seam allowance on the garment when cutting out by folding the pattern back 1cm (⅜in.) on all seam edges.

Topstitching
Do not reverse to fasten off ends of decorative stitching as it spoils the effect of the even stitches. Instead, separate the two layers of fabric, lifting facing from garment for instance, and using a pin or point of unpicker, pull both thread ends out by lifting the loops of stitches. Tie ends firmly in a knot. Trim ends but do not cut close to the fabric.

Thread ends
If thread ends cannot be fastened off neatly by reversing, for example, if you are using contrast colour thread, pull both ends to wrong side of garment, trim and apply a drop of Fray Check liquid.

Group Fourteen: Medium-weight, firm wovens

Linen, viscose/linen, polyester/linen, linen-look fabrics, heavy cotton, raw silk, heavy shantung, silk voile, Thai silk, coarse cotton.

The fabrics in this group fray, but the weight lends itself to crisp structured styles with pleats and topstitching.

Needle – 90 Regular.

Stitch – Straight: 3mm long. Zig-zag: 3.5mm wide, 2mm long.

Thread – Polyester or corespun.

Seams – Open: neaten raw edges with zig-zag. Occasionally it may be advisable to bind raw edges of seams and hems, for instance on an unlined jacket. Flat welt: if the usual machine-fell seam is too bulky, stitch the seam with right sides together, press both edges to one side. Trim under layer to 3mm (⅛in.), neaten remaining edge with zig-zag. Press well. With right side up, topstitch parallel with seam line but within the width of the wider seam allowance.

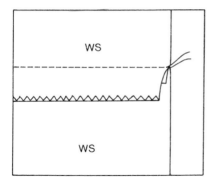

53   *Flat welt seam in medium-weight or bulky fabrics.*

54   *Several rows of stitching make a flat hem on firm medium-weight fabrics.*

Hems and edges – Blind hem: easy to handle from a depth of about 1.5cm (⅝in.). If the raw edge stretches when zig-zagged, use a more open stitch or else zig-zag over a thread that can be pulled up to tighten the edge. Topstitched: two or more rows of machining can be used for a flat, professional-looking hemline. Fold up once and press, zig-zag raw edge then press hard to make a mark. Work all stitching with garment right side up. The hem depth can vary from 1-5cm (⅜-2in.). Wundaweb: suitable for most fabrics in this group but test first to be sure. Hem must be 3cm (1¼in.) deep. Do not press over neatened edge once the Wundaweb is in place. Facings: suitable for all fabrics. Edge stitching may be necessary to flatten the edges. If they still spring up, place small pieces of Wundaweb between garment and facing. Alternatively, make a feature of the facing by attaching it to the wrong side then finishing it on the right side, stitching round the outer edge decoratively.

Fringed fabric
Zig-zag stitch

Edges and hemlines of garments or bags, mats, curtains etc., can be fringed if they are made from plain-weave coarse fabric and if the edge is on the straight grain. Trim the edge cleanly on the grain and fray out the yarns until you have the required depth of fringe. Zig-zag over the yarn beside the fringe with a small stitch. For further emphasis and to make the article firmer zig-zag again but this time over a fine crochet cotton or topstitching thread, perhaps using a contrast colour. To make a border, pull out some more threads a short distance above the fringe and treat each edge in the same way.

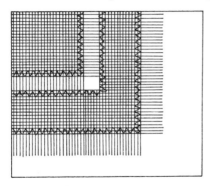
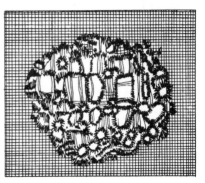

55 *Fringed edge and border on plain-weave coarse fabric.*

56 *Textured 'windows' created by removing threads in one direction.*

Textured windows
Zig-zag stitch

Square shapes could be placed at random or as a border using any coarse, plain-weave fabric. Use matching or toning thread. Mark out a square, snip and remove all threads in one direction within the square. Put the fabric very tautly in a hoop, wrong side up. Use a close, wide zig-zag and stitch round the edge of the square to seal the edges. Within the square, work random stitching over the yarns, drawing them together and separating them.

Textured open panel
Zig-zag stitch

This involves removing threads in both directions from an even-weave fabric, so it is not really robust enough for garments but could be used on bags, cushions etc.

Outline your design shape on the fabric using chalk or fabric pen. Within that area, remove threads in one or both directions, but in patches. Put the fabric tautly in a hoop, right side up. Seal the edge all round with zig-zag in matching thread. The decorative stitching can be shaded or contrasting colours.

Using a medium-size zig-zag, stitch in blocks and patches, partly on the fabric, partly on the open area. Remaining yarns should be stitched over to strengthen the intersection. Cobwebs can be made by stitching back and forth across a space. This decoration is very time-consuming; it takes a lot of stitching to be effective.

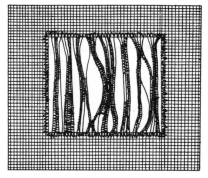

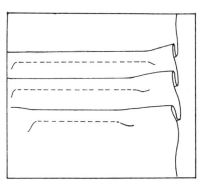

57 *Textured open panel created by removing threads in both directions.*

58 *Feature tucks instead of darts or gathers in plain springy fabric.*

Feature tucks
Straight stitch

On plain, springy fabric, instead of darts in bodice or gathers over a sleeve head, make several tucks of varying lengths. Fold the fabric, wrong sides together, and stitch the width of the foot from the fold. Press the tuck as folded, not flat. Fold the fabric for the next tuck, stitch, press and so on. Make sure that you take up the same amount of fabric as allowed on the pattern for the original shaping. Do not press flat.

Long fringing
Straight stitch, Fringe fork
The wire fork attachment for fringing is a device that has been included with quite basic machines for a long time but not many people get around to using it. Fringe can be added to stoles, rugs, capes, coats and household items such as bath mats can be made by stitching rows close together. Soft yarns of any type or thickness can be used. Some of the modern knitting yarns produce exquisite results. If possible, sew on to a firm backing fabric. If soft fabric is used, turn up the hem first to form a double layer. Use a large straight stitch. Wrap some yarn evenly around the fork at the open end and slide it under the machine foot. Lower the foot across the fork. Stop and gently pull out the fork until nearly all the loops have come off the end.

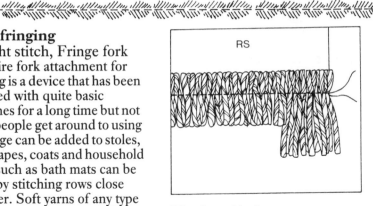

59   *Long fringing.*

Wind some more yarn on the fork from the front and continue. The fringe can be left looped or it can be cut. It can be doubled by cutting both sides and pressing all yarns in one direction. For a fringe with one long edge, use the zip foot so that you can stitch close to one prong of the fork. For tufted areas, cut all loops and then trim short.

Circular stitching
Zig-zag or various automatic stitches. This is fun to do and can be done on mats and hats as well as on garments. Create different effects by changing the thread colour; random-dyed thread is also interesting to use. Soft fabrics and mats should be supported by an appropriate weight of Vilene but firmly woven fabrics will remain flat without support. A special circular stitching accessory is available for most machines but a simple alternative is to attach a drawing pin, point up, to the bed of the machine, using sellotape or basting tape. Line up the pin so that it is level with the needle. The closer it is to the needle the smaller the circle will be. Mark the centre of a circle, push the fabric over the pin, right side up, lower the foot and sew. Try various patterns; some stitches will look like the petals of a flower. Stitches that are not symmetrical give very interesting results. On completion, pull the thread ends to wrong side and fasten off making sure that the join is neat on the right side.

Group Fifteen:
Medium-weight, loose-weave fabric

Wool hopsack, viscose/polyester hopsack, strawcloth, basket-weave wool, folkweave, wool/angora, wool/rabbit, crinkle wool, wool crêpe.

Although soft and open, these fabrics do not usually fray as the yarns are matt, some even hairy, and they remain in place. Take care with pressing as too much moisture will close the spaces between the yarns and shrink the fabric.

Needle – 90 Regular.

Stitch – Straight: 3mm. Zig-zag: 3.5mm wide, 2mm long.

Thread – Mercerized or polyester.

Seams – Open: neaten with zig-zag. Press carefully to avoid imprints. Flat welt: this can look attractive on sporty, unlined jackets etc., possibly in a contrasting colour. Use a larger stitch ie. 4mm (just over ⅛in.) on wool or hairy fabrics.

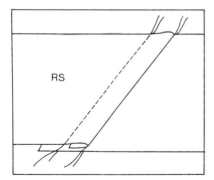

60   *Flat welt seam on medium-weight loose-weave fabrics.*

Hems and edges – Blind hem: suitable for all fabrics. Narrow, machine stitched: on plain fabric and sporty clothes. Facings: lining fabric may be preferable on bulky fabrics.

Wool or fabric border
Straight stitch

A simple border can be added to a dirndl-style skirt made from loosely-woven wool or synthetic fabric such as hopsack, folkweave etc. Select knitting yarns of interesting texture and/or cut narrow strips of fabrics, preferably ones that fray little but which are soft. Place the strips in rows in an attractive arrangement and pin across them at intervals.

Use a colour thread that is unobtrusive and blends with all the colours, use a medium length straight stitch and the zip foot and stitch

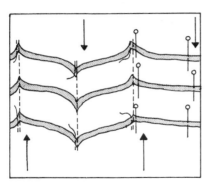

61 *Border on loose-weave fabric using strips of fabric or knitting yarn.*

across the yarns close to the pins. Fasten off the stitching at each end. The rows of stitching can be spaced as you wish, either evenly or unevenly spaced. You will produce a slightly wavy border if you stitch in alternate directions.

Arrowheads

Instead of stitched arrowheads at the tops of pleats and ends of piped pockets cut triangles of suede, leather or suede fabric (buy elbow patches and cut up if scraps are not available). Place in position, secure across one corner with basting tape and stitch all round inside the edge with straight or zig-zag stitch. If you wish, you can decorate the centres before attaching to the garment.

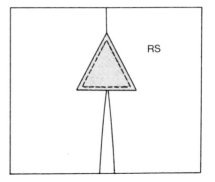

62 *Suede arrowheads.*

Corners in zig-zag

Corners in zig-zag or satin stitch can be open or closed. To make an open corner, stop with the needle on the left when making a left turn. For a closed corner, stop with the needle on the right. If you can vary the width of the zig-zag as you sew, reduce it at an angle of 45 degrees at the corner, turn the work and increase it again to match the first side.

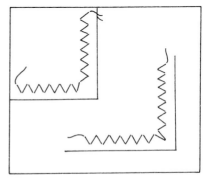

63 *Neat zig-zagging at corners, left: inwards; right: outwards.*

Group Sixteen:
Hard-finish medium to heavy fabric

Proofed poplin, heavy cotton, glazed heavy cotton, proofed glazed cotton, showerproof poplin, showerproof polyester gaberdine, showerproof polyester/cotton, sailcloth, denim, canvas, coated cotton.

These fabrics are firm and closely woven. The surface finish will prevent any easing in of fullness. Seams may wrinkle in some fabrics. If they are difficult to press flat use top stitching to help. Fabrics that are glazed or proofed mark easily; make sure you do not have to unpick.

Needle – 100 Regular or 90 Jeans needle.

Stitch – Straight: 3.5mm. Zig-zag: 3.5mm wide, 2.5mm long.

Thread – Polyester or corespun.

Seams – Open: neaten with zig-zag. Flat welt or welt.

Hems and edges – Machined: finished with one or more rows of stitching at a depth of 1-5cm (3/8-2in.) Most are too firm to turn under twice so zig-zag the raw edge, then press hard to make a line on which to stitch. Wundaweb hem: works well on all fabrics. Facings: suitable for all fabrics, possibly finished decoratively on the right side. If lined, the lining can be taken to the edge and one or more rows of top stitching added to hold back the lining and make the edge firmer.

Ribbing hem

Depending on the type and style of garment cuff, ribbing can be added to ankles as well as cuffs, waist ribbing can be used on jackets and trouser waists and trimmed to add to necklines. Measure length required, stretched, join ends and re-fold with wrong side inside. Insert gathering thread in garment. Slide ribbing over garment, pull up gathers to fit ribbing slightly stretched (test by slipping over ankle, hips

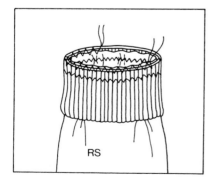

RS

64 *Showing cuff ribbing being attached to sleeve.*

etc.). Stitch to attach, using zig-zag or stretch stitch. Neaten garment edge and both ribbing edges together using a stretch overlock stitch or wide zig-zag. Pull ribbing to extend beyond garment.

Insert wide elastic webbing through trouser waist and pull up to fit. Do the same with ankles etc., if more grip is needed.

Elastic channels
Straight stitch

To make a casing to take elastic, extend the length of the garment by twice (or four times) the width of the elastic plus 3mm (⅛in.) ease and 1cm (⅜in.) seam allowance. If the garment seam slopes, remember to slope the extension edge the other way so that it will lie flat against the garment.

Before stitching the seam, make two dots with fabric pen 1cm (⅜in.) down from the end and 2cm (¾in.) or more (the width of the elastic). Stitch as far as each dot and fasten off. Press open seam; neaten raw edge of garment, fold casing down on to wrong side and press hard. With right side up, stitch beside mark. Thread elastic through slot.

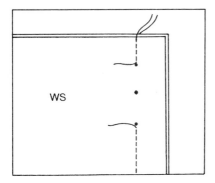 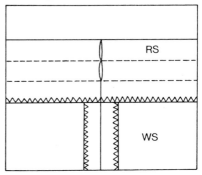

65 *Leaving a gap in the seam for elastic.* **66** *Stitching the hem leaving slots for elastic.*

If you wish to use wide elastic, it is more comfortable and attractive to use narrow elastic and make two channels. Follow the procedure above but leave two gaps 1cm (⅜in.) apart and make two parallel lines of stitching from the right side.

Zip stitching

The smaller the stitch the more likelihood there is that the fabric will wrinkle. Use a large stitch, even the topstitching stitch if your machine has one. On linen-type fabrics, you might topstitch for emphasis, using the same stitch on the zip. Insert the zip by the even-hems method so that the stitching is equidistant from the seam line on both sides.

Marking seam lines

On some glazed, polished or compressed hard-surface fabrics, the machine needle can be used to mark seam lines, guide lines, fold lines, even pocket positions. Set the stitch to a large straight stitch, do not thread up, and stitch the line required through one or two layers of fabric, resulting in a row of holes. This works on fabrics such as taffeta and on some hard-finish cottons.

Pleats

With right sides together, stitch on the seam line, from waist to pleat release point, with normal straight stitch. Fasten off the stitching – reverse, tie-off etc., but without removing the work. Change to a basting stitch or the longest straight stitch and sew on the pleat line to the hem. This gives a perfect base for pressing a knife edge and is easily pulled out when you are ready to turn up the hem.

How to unpick

Straight stitching is easy to undo and will not harm the majority of fabrics. Release the end of the machine stitching by lifting the thread from several stitches using the point of an unpicker or a pin. When you have an end of thread long enough to grasp take hold of it firmly with moist fingers and snap it back quickly and hard against the seam stitching. The thread will break 1cm (3/8in.) or so further down. Turn the seam over, pick up the loose end, lift it clear of the seam and snap it back to break it further along. Continue like this on alternate sides. Do not pull or gather the thread or it will not break. If you encounter resistance, cut the thread and pull out the tight stitches with an unpicker.

On fine or sheer fabrics or in cases where you cannot pick up the thread, use an unpicker and split the seam bit by bit by cutting three or four stitches, tugging the seam edges apart to loosen a few more, cut those stitches, tug the seam apart and so on. Remove all thread ends using the tweezers on your bodkin or, on wool where ends tend to stick, damp your fingers and rub the fabric.

Zig-zag, satin stitch and embroidery are difficult to unpick. Do it one stitch at a time.

Press the fabric after unpicking, the heat helps to close up the holes.

Group Seventeen: Fine, silky knits

Plain and printed polyester jersey, fine acrylic jersey, silk jersey, warp-knit jersey, nylon jersey, acetate jersey.

Some of these fabrics ladder, so edges should be handled with care. Cut all pieces lying in one direction as they can shade, especially plain fabrics. Check which direction ladders run on one edge and cut pieces so that ladders run down the hem not into the garment.

Needle – 70 Ballpoint or Universal.

Stitch – Straight: 2mm long and pull the fabric slightly or 3mm stretch stitch or slight zig-zag. Zig-zag 3mm wide, 2mm long.

Thread – Polyester, corespun if missed stitches occur.

Seams – Open: use on all fabrics but edges may curl up. Neaten if required with an open decorative stitch to hold flat. If seams wrinkle, stretch out on pressing surface and pin at each end. Cut narrow strips of Wundaweb and slide them under each seam allowance. Press well and allow to cool before moving. Flat welt: suitable for certain seams on some garments.

Hems and edges – Narrow, stitched hems: these look good on all fabrics. Turn up fabric once 3mm-1cm (⅛-⅜in.). Stitch from right side with several rows of straight stitch or one row of zig-zag or open decorative stitch. Trim surplus from wrong side. Binding: suitable for all fabrics; finish binding on right side with decorative stitch. Facings: edges of garment may need topstitching to prevent facings popping out. Alternatively try small pieces of Wundaweb between facing and garment.

If you encounter missed stitches, change to a Universal needle which has a longer scarf and holds the thread against it better; change to a smaller size stitch, narrower zig-zag etc., and place the fabric on paper or Stitch-n-Tear to prevent it from being pushed into the needle hole. Also, often, a change to a cotton-covered thread, such as Duet, will help to reduce the static.

Fluted pin-tucks
Zig-zag

A decorative feature suitable for thin, soft fabrics.

Plan a design of small, parallel, diagonal tucks or a diamond design and mark the centre of the area. Fold the fabric on the cross 1-2cm (⅜-¾in.) from the centre with wrong sides together and press the crease. Using a small zig-zag stitch, sew along the fold just catching the fabric when the needle swings to the left. Fold the second tuck at right angles to the first for diamonds, the same distance from the centre, press and

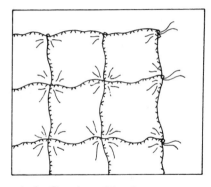

67 *Fluted pin tucks on thin soft fabric.*

stitch. Continue like this, working round the centre or for parallel tucks, in the same direction using an adjustable marker set at a distance of 2-4cms (¾-1½in.). The fact that the crease is on the cross makes the fold stretch and flute slightly. This decoration looks attractive worked in a contrasting thread on plain fabric, as a central design on a blouse front, sleeve head, back of a robe, on cushions made of satin etc. It is also very effective on lightweight synthetic jersey. Pull the fabric as you stitch to produce more fluting. The stitch may appear uneven on jersey so use matching thread.

Flat stitched hem

This is suitable for all jersey fabrics but it is also useful on plain woven fabrics. Turn up and press a single fold at the edge of the garment 1-2cm (⅜-¾in.) deep. Select an open stitch such as honeycomb or elastic stitch and stitch along the fold with the needle only just on the fabric when it moves to the right. Work another row against the first. Trim off surplus on wrong side. If the stitching draws up the fabric, place a narrow strip of Stitch-n-Tear inside the fold.

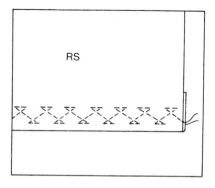

68 *Flat hem finished with open decorative stitch.*

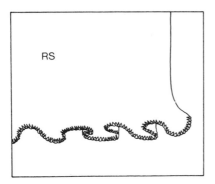

69 *Fluted edge on jersey fabric.*

Fluted edge

A popular way of finishing jersey. Trim the garment to 5mm (¼in.) longer than needed. Set the machine to a small close zig-zag. Fold the edge of the fabric under and feed it under the foot. Zig-zag over the fold but stretch the fabric as much as possible. Stitch in short bursts to keep an even pull on the fabric. Trim off the surplus raw edge on the wrong side.

Shell edges

These are suitable for most fine fabrics but are especially suitable for light and medium-weight jersey. Fold under the edge of the fabric, select a stitch that throws one zig-zag to the right, use maximum width or a little less and stitch inside the folded edge with the zig-zag off the edge. Trim surplus fabric from the wrong side. To increase the shell tighten the upper tension a little.

Tucks can be made by shell edging along a fold, adding more parallel tucks as required. Press in one direction or press pairs outwards and

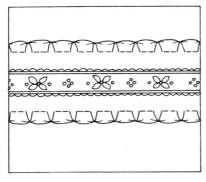

70 *Using shell tucks and ribbon on cuffs, tabs and bands.*

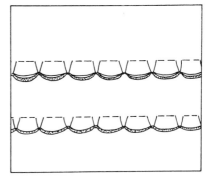

71 *Shell tucks with narrow strips of fine jersey added to the edge.*

place a line of ribbon or braid between them. Attach the braid with a stitch that echoes the shells. Cuffs, tabs or band fastenings can be edged with shell stitch. Buttonholes placed vertically in a strap could be covered with braid, leaving the edge unstitched beside each buttonhole to make a decorative fly opening.

Rolled shell hems are made using the shell hem foot with a zig-zag stitch. Practise on spare fabric first to get the hang of feeding in the fabric.

Contrast edging of jersey fabric can be added by placing a second strip of fabric folded in half with the fold extending beyond the hem fold by 2-3mm (^{1}/16-^{1}/8in.). Work the shell stitch as before and the outer edge is drawn in. This can be done on woven fabric provided the folded edging is jersey. A further alternative is to place fine cord against the folded edge of the hem. The shell stitch catches the cord with each zig-zag.

A garment edge can be faced with contrast fabric and shell edged at the same time. Use a wide piece of fabric, fold it, place under the main hem and shell edge. Further in on the wrong side, turn under the raw edge of the contrast and stitch down.

Openwork insertion can be made by making corded scallops along two edges of fabric; placing them together edge to edge and joining the centres of each pair of scallops with a bar tack.

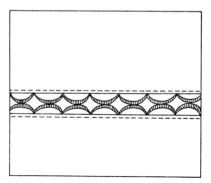

72 *Openwork insertion made by joining two rows of corded scallops.*

Neatening edges

If your machine has a one-sided foot with a little wire extending from the base, use this for zig-zagging stretchy fabrics. The wire prevents the edge from shrinking back under the needle.

Reverse appliqué

This produces a firm result. Use for bolero, waistcoat, sleeves, bedcover, bag etc. Use 4 layers of soft, lightweight fabrics, one or even two can be thin synthetic jersey. The top layer should be a transparent

fabric such as net. Place all layers together using a soft, firm-woven fabric on the underneath to avoid the necessity for using paper. Pin the layers at intervals. Mark out a random design using fabric pen; avoid angles and corners. Do not tack.

Use a medium-width, close zig-zag stitch and normal sewing thread; stitch the design stopping as few times as possible. Do not overlap ends of stitching or it looks lumpy. Remove pins where possible. On completion, carefully trim away 1, 2 or occasionally 3 layers of fabric in each part of the design.

Satin stitching – buttonholes etc

Fabric can jam and stop feeding through without you noticing immediately. Can be caused by uneven thickness, the foot failing to rise over a bulky edge or seam, even a knot of basting thread can be the reason. Trim all ends of thread, cut off knots, removing basting if possible, watch the stitching carefully and keep the fabric moving. If layers are particularly uneven put paper or Stitch-n-Tear beneath the fabric, tearing it away on completion.

Missed stitches

This is a common and extremely irritating problem which occurs most often on synthetic jersey and which has a number of possible solutions, each of which should be tried. See page 24: Stitch distortion.

Seam stitching

To begin stitching, insert fabric under the foot, lower the needle, lower the foot and stitch. (The exception to this is with fully electronic machines.)

Group Eighteen: Medium-weight knits

Sweater rib, acrylic knit, bouclé knit, lacy knits, raschel knit, mesh fabric.

These fabrics vary in thickness and construction, some are firm and open, others stretch a lot in one or both directions. Those that become baggy in wear may recover their shape or may have to be pressed. They do not fray but lumps may fall from cut edges.

Needle – 90-100 Ballpoint.

Stitch – Straight or stretch stitch: 3mm long. Zig-zag: 4mm wide, 3mm long.

Thread – Polyester.

Seams – Narrow: stitch once, trim and zig-zag or overlock or use one row of open, stretch stitch to hold seam and neaten. Flat welt: use for emphasis on yokes, raglan seams etc. If fabrics stretch across width to double their size when stretched hard, place a piece of tape or bias binding along shoulder and waist seams and stitch through it. Cut the tape exactly to size, taking the measurement from the paper pattern. A neater outline results if this is also done round armholes, crutch seams etc. If fabric is bulky, stitch the seam then stitch the tape close beside it.

Hems and edges – Narrow machined: fold up fabric once 5mm (¼in.) and stitch with open, decorative stitch, honeycomb, zig-zag etc. If edge stretches, place on paper or insert a thread to be pulled up. Sweater ribs may be straight stitched except for necklines. Ribbing or bias edge: suitable for all fabrics. Blind hem: suitable for all fabrics but for added strength to withstand stretching, use zig-zag stitch instead of blind stitch. Facings: suitable for lightweight flat knits only.

Hand-sewn hems in soft fabrics

When neatening the raw edge before hand sewing with catch stitch, correct possible stretching and fluting by zig-zagging over a thick thread (or double sewing thread) and pulling it up.

Satin stitch

Some fabrics are inclined to slip or fail to be gripped by the feed teeth when doing satin stitch and buttonholes particularly. If it fails to feed and stitches accumulate in one place when you do the trial run, put paper or Stitch-n-Tear beneath it.

Gathered or eased seams

When stitching seams with shaping included, have the fuller side of the fabric uppermost in the machine and stitch slowly, using the point of your bodkin or small scissors to flatten and divide gathers or puckers of fabric. With a heavily-gathered edge it helps, in addition, to pull the fabric taut with the left hand, at right angles to the foot.

Shaped seams, top-stitching, decorative stitching

When stopping to re-position the fabric in a long run of stitching, always stop with the needle down in the fabric to prevent movement. Your machine may have a needle up/down button that you can press before you start. If it is a machine that always stops with the needle in the up position, tap the foot control, press the button once or do whatever is necessary to lower the needle. On basic machines, turn the balance wheel towards you until you see the needle enter the fabric.

Reversing at ends of seams

Seam ends will usually be trimmed at a later stage so reverse the stitching 1-1.5cm (³/₈ to ⁵/₈in.) inside the raw edge and the seam will not come apart at the end after trimming.

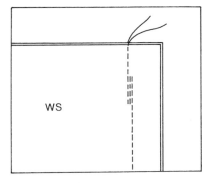

74 *Reversing inside edge to secure seam end.*

Keeping zip sides level

Before inserting the zip, machine a marker across the tape ends above the top stops. Snip the thread between the tapes. Insert the zip by the required method placing the marker stitching at the same level on each side of the opening.

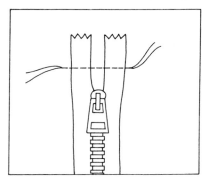

75 *Marker in place across zip.*

Group Nineteen: Medium-weight pile knits

Stretch towelling, suede fabric, Ultra-suede, jersey-backed suede, fine velour, panné velvet.

With the exception of towelling these fabrics must all be cut with the pile running in one direction from hem upwards. Pieces of pile fall from cut edges, especially towelling, but it does not continue. The more stretch in the fabric the more care is needed.

Needle – 90 Ballpoint.

Stitch – Straight: 3mm but slightly pull the fabric or use a stretch stitch. Zig-zag: 3mm wide, 3mm long.

Thread – Polyester.

Seams – Narrow: zig-zag both raw edges together, or use one row of stitching such as overlock, pullover etc. Flat welt: good on suede fabric but the extra stitching on stretch towelling often stretches the seam and it cannot be pressed flat. Open seams: these can be used on velour and panné velvet but on others the edges may curl up.

Hems and edges – Machined hem: suitable on all fabrics; do not turn under the raw edge. If available, use a stretch stitch. Avoid facings, substitute a double fabric edge, see page 95.

Monogram
Zig-zag stitch

Initials can be stitched using satin stitch or any suitable pattern on the machine. Depending on your machine, you may be able to choose one pattern and lengthen it to fit the size of the letters, or use a small pattern and let it repeat as necessary. Alternatively use the zig-zag closed up and stitch each part of the letters, narrowing the stitch if possible at each end.

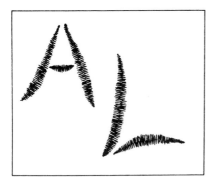

76 *Monogram using lengthened automatic pattern.*

Draw the letters on the right side of the fabric and put Stitch-n-Tear underneath. On completion, pull thread ends to wrong side to fasten off.

Monograms are particularly effective on pile fabrics and towelling. Support the fabric with Stitch-n-Tear, draw the letters on another piece and place it on top of the fabric to flatten the pile. Stitch monogram and carefully remove Stitch-n-Tear from both sides.

Letters on check fabric

Zig-zag stitch. Mark out letters on the fabric using the checks to make square shapes. Using a contrasting thread and a very small zig-zag stitch loosen the top tension. Stitch with right side up to produce a nubbly, bouclé effect outline.

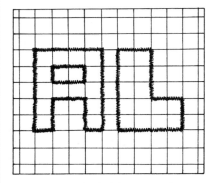

77 *Using check fabric to outline letters.*

Matching seams

For careful, accurate matching, when attaching a collar for example, baste in place, then secure at centre back and centre front positions with 1-2cm (3/8-3/4in.) of machine stitching on the seam line. Stitch all round in the usual way and there is no fear of matched points moving.

Pins

If you pin-baste a seam ie. omit thread-basting and machine over the pins, use only steel-headed pins; the machine foot will not ride over coloured plastic heads.

Pinning seams

Many straight seams without shaping or gathers in non-slippery fabrics can be pinned ready for stitching instead of basting with thread. Pin layers together with fabric flat on the table to avoid distortion, insert pins with heads extending over raw edges, pick up fabric at seam line position only and do not push in pins too far.

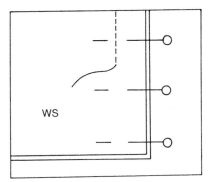

78 *Pin basting; stitching over pins.*

Group Twenty: Heavy pile knits

Velour, track-suit fabric, acrylic velour, jersey-backed chenille, jersey-backed velvet and velveteen, brushed acrylic knit, jersey velour, poodle cloth, Tricel velour.

These fabrics must all be cut with the pile running one way, that is from hem to top. Lumps of pile fall from cut edges but this will not continue. Dual feed is invaluable to stop creeping but otherwise they are easy to handle.

Needle – 100 Regular. 100 Ballpoint for knit.

Stitch – Straight: 4mm long but pull knit fabrics slightly or use stretch stitch. Zig-zag: 4mm wide; 3mm long.

Thread – Polyester.

Seams – Open: neaten edges with zig-zag, open stitch, overlock etc.

Hems and edges – Blind hem stitch: works well as fabrics are bulky. Machined hem: attractive on some garments. Use matching thread so stitches create an indentation. Use straight stitch or an open stitch such as honeycomb. Facings: in most cases they will be too bulky. Lining fabric is not suitable as it is fine and will work out of the garment. Substitute ribbing, a bias edge (page 95) or bind the edges using woven contrasting fabric.

Corded Hem
Straight stitch, grooved foot.

An interesting way of finishing hems on medium and heavy woven fabrics as well as on heavy, woven pile fabrics. Use a 3 groove foot, large twin needle and thick wool as a filler for the tucks. Set the machine to a large, straight stitch. Fold up the hem, baste and press. With right side up stitch one or two pin tucks starting 1cm (³⁄₈in.) or more inside the garment edge. More tucks make the edge rigid which is not suitable for

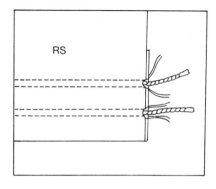

79   *Corded hem using twin needle.*

hemlines but you may want to make use of this on the edges of a heavy cape, bedcover, rug or bag. On completion, trim away surplus fabric close to stitching. Press right side down on a folded towel. On right side press up to but not over the tucks.

Machine needle

If the needle makes a popping sound in the fabric, it is either blunt or too big a size for the material.

Easing

The technique for easing one layer when sewing a shaped or curved seam is to put the fabric under the foot with the bigger piece on top, stitch the seam slowly, in short bursts, but using both forefingers to pull the fabric outwards and at the same time pushing the top layer towards the needle to ease in the fullness. It does not help to pin the seam unless it is very curved but you need a couple of matching points. This can be done by snipping each edge separately at the quarter and halfway points before putting the edges together.

If there is only a slight amount of ease to be included or if the seam is on the straight grain, snip the edge of the shorter piece at intervals. Also make matching points on both pieces using fabric pen. Place the edges together and put under the machine foot with the short piece uppermost, anchor the end of the seam with a few stitches then sew forwards quite fast but holding the upper layer with both hands and stretching it to fit the under layer. Both seams should be snipped again before pressing.

Threading

If the reel of thread has a notch in the end for holding the cut end, be sure to place it on the machine with the notch away from the direction of threading so that the thread does not get caught.

Pinning

Always insert pins at an angle, even at right angles, to the seam. The fabric does not pucker at each pin and it keeps a larger area flat.

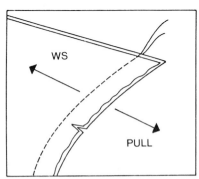

WS

PULL

80 *Pull fabric outwards when easing one layer on to the other.*

Group Twenty-one: Lightweight matt jersey

Cotton jersey, acrylic jersey, cotton/modal jersey.

These vary in thickness, they stretch a great deal across the width but are not difficult to sew.

Needle – 70 Ballpoint or Universal.

Stitch – Straight: 2mm and pull the fabric slightly. Zig-zag: 3mm wide, 2 mm long.

Thread – Polyester.

Seams – Narrow: either use an open zig-zag stitch to sew the seam and neaten it, or straight stitch and then make firm edges with zig-zag or overlock. The latter is more bulky. Open: these can be used on dresses if necessary but edges tend to curl up. Flat welt: stitch once, trim both edges and press to one side. Stitch beside seam from right side with zig-zag or decorative stitch.

Hems and edges – Blindstitch hem: difficult to control in thin fabrics. confine it to a depth of 2cm (¾in.) Machined hem: turn up once and stitch with one or more rows of straight or decorative stitch. Place on paper if fabric stretches across the width while being stitched. Fluted hem: suitable for all fabrics.

Bias edging
Straight stitch.

This is an attractive contrast edging for necklines and sleeve edges in silk or satin and applied to matt or hairy fabrics.

Cut bias strips of contrast fabric 3cm (1¼in.) wide or whatever is required. Fold in half wrong side inside and press. Place on right side of garment with fold extending over garment and stitch in place taking 5mm (¼in.) seam allowance on the bias strip but the usual amount on the garment. Trim garment seam allowance level with bias edges and

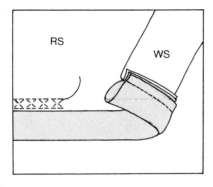

81 *Bias edging using contrasting fabric, stitched flat to finish.*

neaten all three together. Use an open stitch; there will be little or no fraying so zig-zag is unnecessary, the stitching is more for keeping the three edges together. Pull the bias strip so that it extends beyond the garment and press the join. If the fabric is such that it does not lie flat, add a row of stitching through garment and seam allowances, beside the seam. Straight stitch can be used although a symmetrical, decorative stitch such as honeycomb looks attractive.

Group Twenty-two: Firm, face-finish wovens

Flannel, facecloth, doeskin, camel cloth, beavercloth, blazercloth.

These fabrics have a one-way brushed surface that is sometimes difficult to determine but they must all be cut with the pieces in one direction, usually running down. On the whole, the fabrics will not fray.

Needle – 90 or 100 Regular.

Stitch – Straight: 4mm long. Zig-zag: 3mm wide, 2.5mm long.

Thread – Polyester or mercerized.

Seams – Open: neaten raw edges with zig-zag but not if garment is to be lined. Flat welt: looks good on all these fabrics.

Hems and edges – Blindstitch hem: good on all fabrics. Topstitched hems: one or two lines of stitching may be suitable to secure hems of all depths, provided it looks right on the garment. Facings: suitable for coats, jackets etc.

Soutache braid
Straight stitch. Foot with central hole if possible.

A decorative edging that is useful for holding down facings or hems. Make sure you have Vilene on the back of the garment and turn in and baste the hem or facing in place. Outline the required design using tailor's chalk or chalk pencil, avoiding angles if possible. Using thread to match the braid and a medium-size stitch to enable full control, feed the braid under the foot and stitch, lining up the hole in the front of the foot with the centre of the braid. On the wrong side trim excess fabric to 2cm (¾in.) from the stitching and zig-zag it if the garment is unlined. Press carefully up to the braid but not over it.

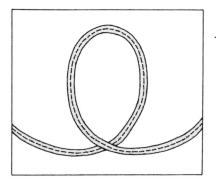

82 *Soutache braid attached to firm fabric.*

Geometric couching
Zig-zag stitch.

This can be worked on any firm coating, suiting, linen, wool etc. as a border at hems, cuffs and front edges, curtains, cushions. Select three bright contrasting colours of fine crochet cotton, topstitch thread or embroidery thread and sewing thread to match each one. The following measurements make a border 8cm (3in.) deep. Using tailor's chalk or fabric pen rule a line for the middle row of couching and mark every 5cm (2in.). Draw lines at right angles at each point 5cm (2in.) long. Join up alternate points. Attach cording foot if possible and insert cord, set machine to a small zig-zag that will just straddle the cord and stitch along the line turning at right angles at each point as follows. Stop at the corner with the needle down on the same side at the right angle turns, ie. inside the angle. Lift the foot, turn the fabric, lower the foot and continue. As the foot is lowered, the cord is pulled taut.

Change the colour of cord and thread and work the second row parallel with the first, using the edge of the foot as a guide. Repeat for the third row on the other side of the first.

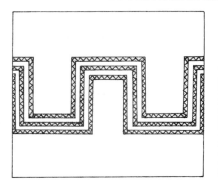

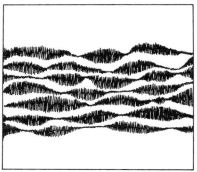

83 *Geometric couched design.*   84 *Self-colour texture using varying zig-zag stitch.*

Self-colour texture
Zig-zag stitch.

This is a simple but very effective decoration for plain coating, flannel etc. Work panels of zig-zag in lines, varying the width of the stitch. Use thread to match the fabric and leave small spaces between the rows. Loosen the top tension and close up the stitch but not quite to satin stitch.

Thread ends

When sewing in a circle, for instance round the armhole to set in a sleeve, or zig-zagging to neaten, start stitching, then stop and cut off the thread ends. Continue stitching, overlapping the start of the line by 1cm (³⁄₈in.) or so. This makes a smoother join and there is no chance of tangled thread ends or a heavy knot of thread.

Buttonholes

Before stitching, place a small piece of Wundaweb between the garment and the facing and press. This provides a firmer base on which to stitch and it also lessens the chance of fraying after the buttonholes are cut.

Edge stitching

Fold under raw edge of fabric and press, do not baste. Place under machine with right side up so that narrow edge is clamped flat against machine bed and cannot curl over. Stitch on the fold or just inside. Press the stitching. On wrong side carefully trim off raw edge close to stitching.

Seam stitching

When sewing long seams, prevent fabric grain distortion and stop the upper layer from creeping forward by lifting both layers up at an angle in front of the foot, off the machine bed.

Lapel stitching

When topstitching a collar and lapel, establish the roll line position where the rever breaks, stitch on the outside of the garment from hem to break line (roughly at top button). Remove work and turn over, continue stitching lapel and collar from the other side to ensure the stitch is identical throughout. Sew in ends between the layers, dealing with the ends at the break line before starting the final stitching.

Seam stitching

Always stitch just beside your line of basting, to the outside of the seam line. This prevents basting thread becoming entangled with machining and makes the removal of the basting easier and quicker as well as ensuring that machining is not pulled.

Direction of stitching

Always stitch with the angle of the seam, that is from wide to narrow, which is from hem to waist or neck or from underarm to wrist, crutch to ankle etc. This eliminates puckering, dragging of seams and distortion of grain. Even when zig-zagging to neaten a raw edge, it is best to do it in the right direction so that you are smoothing rather than ruffling the ends of fraying yarns. It also prevents stretching and fluting of raw edges.

Group Twenty-three: Firm, woven, pile fabrics

Corduroy, needlecord, velveteen.

In addition to fraying of the backing yarns, these fabrics also shed tufts of pile when cut.

Cut out all pieces with pile running from hem upwards and stitch all seams in the same direction. The woven backing varies in softness but none are difficult to handle. Dual feed is invaluable for preventing creeping of pile.

Needle – 90 Regular or Jeans needle on cords.

Stitch – Straight: 3.5mm long. Zig-zag: 2.5mm wide, 2mm long.

Thread – Polyester or corespun.

Seams – Open: neaten with zig-zag. Seams on straight grain may cockle. Flat welt: good on cords.

Hems and edges – Blind hem: successful on all pile fabrics. Machined: zig-zag raw edges and turn up once. Stitch with one or more rows but do not place first row too near fold as the pile creates a deceptive outer edge. Facings: use lining to reduce bulk. Stitched edges: necklines and even armholes can be zig-zagged and turned in 3-5mm (⅛-¼in.) and finished with straight or zig-zag stitch. Decorative stitches: hems can be finished with an open zig-zag stitch such as feather stitch or honeycomb. Use a matching or lighter shade of thread to give an attractive compressed border.

Couching
Zig-zag stitch; foot with central hole if available.

Metallic thread or metal-with-fibre thread, crochet yarn or fine knitting yarn makes a stunning decoration for velveteen. Plan to stitch a hem

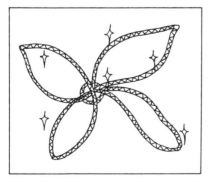 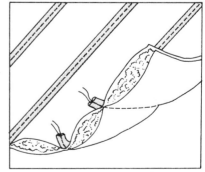

85 *Metallic thread couched on to pile fabric is effective.* **86** *Using narrow ribbon for quilting.*

edge border or a free-style motif (not too small). Thread machine with thread to match the fabric and set it to a small zig-zag, adjusting it to a width suitable to straddle the yarn. Feed the yarn through the hole in the foot or, if not available, see page 34 for an alternative. Work the couching after cutting out and fitting but before facings etc. are complete. Stitch with fabric right side up and no backing material. To make a border, stitch the first line parallel with seam line or hem fold line then use machine foot to guide subsequent parallel lines. To stitch a motif mark a simple outline using chalk pencil and stitch round it. The fabric will bubble if areas are too small. More stitching can be added in parallel rows or random shapes.

Quilting with narrow ribbon
Straight stitch

This is effective on velveteen but it adds bulk to an already bulky fabric so confine it to small areas such as yokes, deep cuffs, fronts of waistcoat, hat or bag.

The quilting is done using narrow 3mm ($\frac{1}{8}$in.) satin ribbon in various colours. Mark out the shape of the piece but do not cut to size. Baste the velveteen right side up on a layer of wadding. If the garment is not to be lined, place a piece of lining or thin cotton beneath the wadding and baste through all three. Alternatively, an odd piece of quilted fabric could be added for extra padding. On the right side mark parallel lines on the bias 4-5cm (1$\frac{1}{2}$-2in.) apart. Use chalk pencil or tailor's chalk. Attach a quilting or short-toe foot to the machine or a perspex see-through foot. Begin in the middle of the fabric, remove basting stitches that are near the first line, feed the ribbon under the foot and stitch down the centre with a small straight stitch. The ribbon and velveteen are both inclined to slip if too big a stitch is used.

Gathering threads
Avoid unsightly, lumpy reversing at the start of gathering threads by working one row of large straight stitches along the seam line, turn and make 2 stitches at right angles, turn and make a second row of gathering thread parallel with the first and closer to the raw edge. To gather, pull up both bobbin ends together.

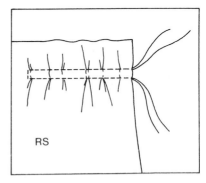

87 *Two rows of gathering thread secured at one end.*

101

Group Twenty-four: Bulk, soft fabrics

Mohair, mohair/wool, reversible coating, moufflin.

These fabrics, although soft, often take some getting used to as they tend not to leave their essentially flat state. Use machine stitching to hold in place and break the surface. If mohair has long pile, cut pieces one-way, pile down.

Needle – 90 Regular. 100 Regular for coating.

Stitch – Straight: 4.5mm long. Zig-zag: 4mm long, 3mm wide.

Thread – Polyester or mercerized.

Seams – Open: zig-zag edges (difficult on mohair). Flat welt: use on coatings, probably with no need to zig-zag the raw edge on the wrong side. Reversible seams: for double cloth only. Separate the layers and snip the connecting thread. Sometimes you may be able to pull long threads out which will release the layers along a straight edge. Stitch two of the layers right sides together, stitch and press open. Fold in the other edges to meet each other over the seam. Baste flat and join with a wide zig-zag or honeycomb stitch or using slip stitch by hand.

Hems and edges – Binding: use bias woven fabric or satin binding on mohair; twill or knitted folded braid can be used on all fabrics. Slide binding over freshly-cut edge and baste through all layers. With garment right side up and using a wide zig-zag stitch, sew the braid to the garment. The stitch should overlap on to the garment sufficiently to hold it securely. Interesting effects can be created by using thread to match the braid, even a more decorative stitch making it look as if the braid has a fancy edge. Reversible hem: separate the layers as for a seam, fold in the edges to meet each other and slipstitch. Often an added row of topstitching will make the edge firmer.

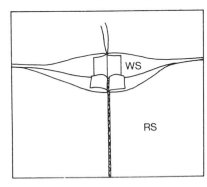

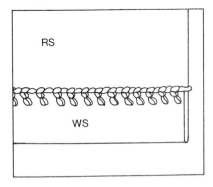

88 *Joining the layers of reversible fabric to make a seam.*

89 *Blanket hem – fabric folded on to right side.*

Blanket hem

A decorative hem for thick fabrics that are firm and fairly non-fraying such as reversible cloth, camel cloth and felt. Can be used on unlined coat and jacket sleeves and hems, stoles and blankets and rugs. One line of stitching holds and neatens.

Wind bobbin with matching or contrasting colour wool. Loosen tension.

Use normal sewing thread in top and tighten tension.

Select a stretch or pullover stitch that sews a straight line and throws out diagonals to one side.

Fold the hem once on to the *right* side, baste. Press heavily until the raw edge makes a mark that is visible on the wrong side. With fabric *wrong* side up stitch along the mark so that the side stitches extend towards the hem.

Stitching a circle to a straight or concave edge

This seam is often needed when making a hat or bag. The edge of the circle will easily stretch and should be at least 2cm (¾in.) shorter than the hat band or bag end. It also tends to slip over the straight edge so start by trimming the circle seam allowance to 1cm (⅜in.) Fold the circle and make dots with fabric pen on the wrong side 1cm (⅜in.) within the raw edge, dividing the edge into 6 or 8 segments. Divide and mark the straight edge in the same way but putting the dots on the right side 3mm (⅛in.) within the raw edge. Place the pieces together and pin at the quarter points. Stitch the seam slowly, carefully matching the dots and easing in the circle to prevent it from stretching – use the point of a bodkin. Remove the pins before you come to them.

Bias seams

Use polyester thread such as *Drima*, which has maximum stretch. Either adjust the stitch to a slight zig-zag, less than ½ on the dial, or loosen the top tension slightly and use a small straight stitch. If the seam bubbles unduly, put tissue paper underneath it and gently remove it afterwards.

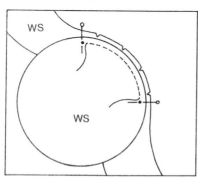

90 *Joining curved edge to straight edge.*

Group Twenty-five: Multi-layer fabrics

Quilting, heavy cloqué, jacquards with several sets of floats which create spaces between layers.

These fabrics are bulky and may not be easily shaped.

Needle – 100 Regular.

Stitch – Straight: 4mm long. Zig-zag: 3mm wide, 2mm wide.

Thread – Polyester or mercerized.

Seams – Narrow: stitch with right sides together, ease wadding from edges, trim and zig-zag to neaten. Flat welt: press seam allowances to one side, trim the under edge to 3mm (⅛in.), neaten the upper edge with zig-zag. With right side up, stitch parallel with seam but through seam allowance with straight or zig-zag stitch. If quilting has no backing fabric, omit the neatening and line the garment.

Hems and edges – Facings: use lining or a plain lightweight fabric. Binding: use bias strips of plain fabric or bought bias binding or twill weave braid. Net: jacquards can be faced with net instead of fabric.

Adding interest to quilting
Straight stitch

Pre-quilted fabric can have additional lines of stitching added to emphasise cuffs, yokes etc. Either use a perfectly matching thread and stitch or use a deliberate contrast such as white or metal thread and zig-zag.

91 *Quilting by stitching on printed fabric.*   **92** *Quilting floral fabric.*

If you quilt your own fabric, sandwich a thin layer of wadding between the fabric and thin cotton or lining fabric. Baste together in rows. If the fabric is plain, mark parallel rows or diamonds using tailor's chalk or chalk pencil. Traditionally the stitch is straight but there is no reason why it should not be decorative. If you use printed fabric use the design on which to quilt. It can be striped, chevron striped, a print of triangles or geometrics. Even if it is floral the motif could be outlined. Alternatively, on plain fabric, outline a motif and stitch with matching or contrasting thread and straight stitch. This feature could be placed centrally on the back of a robe, yoke of a dress etc. Always quilt before cutting the fabric to size.

Don't set yourself too much to do. Plan a design that you can add to until it is sufficient, rather than starting to cover whole areas and finding that the quilting makes it too stiff or that it is taking too long to do.

Angled seams

Stitch angled seams in two stages as follows, never attempt to pivot at the angle as it results in puckers.

Mark the exact corner point on the wrong side of both pieces of fabric. Matching the points and with right sides together, stitch from the point to the end of the seam. Fasten off thread ends. Press the seam open, neaten the raw edges. At the corner, snip the seam allowance of the piece, cut inwards: snip precisely to the end of stitching. Swivel the snipped piece until the raw edges of the second part of the seam are level. Baste together, then stitch, starting at the corner, at the end of the first row, and sewing out to the end of the seam.

93 *Angled seam: stitch from corner point to outer edge.*

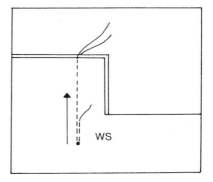

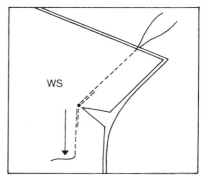

94 *Angled seam: stitch from end of previous stitching to the outer edge.*

Group Twenty-six: Thick loop pile fabrics

Terry towelling, thick towelling, bouclé coating, jersey backed bouclé.

These fabrics can be awkward because of their bulk. Allow extra at seams when cutting out or open seams may not lie flat.

Needle – 100 Regular.

Stitch – Straight: 4mm long. Zig-zag: 4mm wide, 3mm long.

Thread – Corespun.

Seams – Open seams: neaten with zig-zag. Flat welt: good for all fabrics but may not always suit the style of garment.

Hems and edges – Machine hem: zig-zag raw edges and fold up once, to a depth of at least 2cm (¾in.), more if possible. Hold with straight or zig-zag stitch, one row only, more makes the hem stand out. Blind hem: suitable for all but difficult to judge the width of the stitch if reverse side of fabric has pile. Facings: use on coats etc., but avoid on towelling robes. Use narrow bands stitched down or a narrow hem held down with running zig-zag or similar.

Bar tacks

Some machines have an automatic facility for making bar tacks for use on openings, zips and for attaching belt loops. An alternative method is to make four stitches with a maximum-width, close zig-zag, then turn the work and stitch over the top in the other direction with a narrow, close zig-zag.

Belt loops

Make a cord of six strands of fine cord or bold thread, place on paper and stitch over it with a narrow zig-zag. Remove the paper, cut off lengths as required, knotting the ends and passing them through seams to be securely anchored.

Zip-pressing

After stitching, remove all basting, tailor tacks etc., then press the stitching on the wrong side of the garment before turning it over to press the right side. Run the toe of the iron over the stitching to smooth it. Do not put the iron on the zip itself or the fabric will become marked.

Even layers

The appearance of a stitch will vary if the thickness of the fabric varies. Maintain an even thickness for topstitching, decorative stitching etc., by placing pieces of paper or Stitch-n-Tear underneath when required.

Group Twenty-seven:
Medium and heavy flat wovens

Suiting, coating, tweed, worsted, Donegal tweed, gaberdine, twill.

Not difficult to sew but require a heavier touch especially in pressing. The joy of sewing these fabrics is that they can be shaped while warm from the iron and they take good pleats etc.

Needle – 100 Regular.

Stitch – Straight: 4mm long. Zig-zag: 4mm wide, 3mm long.

Thread – Mercerized, polyester or corespun.

Seams – Open: omit neatening or neaten partially if lined. Flat welt: suitable for coats and style features.

Hems and edges – Blind hem: make hems at least 3cm (1¼in.) deep to weight the garment. Narrow machined: turn in 1.5cm (½in.) and press, stitch with parallel rows of straight stitching. Suitable for sleeves, zip edges. Facings: use fabric on outer garments but waistcoats etc., can be lined to the edge and then topstitched.

Corded tucks
Straight stitch, pin-tuck foot.

Smooth finish. Plain wovens are a good base for parallel tucks on collar, yoke, cuffs, pockets etc. Mark out shape of piece but cut larger. Mark centre of piece and draw a line in a suitable position for the first tuck ie. parallel with yoke edge or outer edge if collar. Use a medium thickness crochet cotton as a filler, attach a 5 or 7 groove pin-tuck foot and thread up with machine embroidery thread. Using a 2-3mm (¹⁄₁₆-¹⁄₈in.) stitch sew the first tuck. Make subsequent tucks either at regular intervals using the grooves or graduated, using the full width of the foot as the first space and gradually reducing the distance.

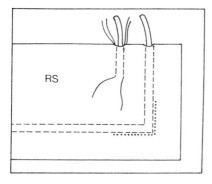

95 *Corded tucks using twin needle: mark angles and corners.*

To turn corners on a collar, sew to the corner, stop with needle down, turn work half way round, take one stitch, turn collar fully and continue with subsequent rows, turn the corners in line with the first. It helps to mark the angle on the collar before you start.

Mitred corners

Fold in and press the two adjacent raw edges. Open out, fold with the adjacent edges together and press. Open out. Locate the two diagonal creases, fold the fabric right sides together and adjacent edges together and stitch along the crease. Trim off the corners, turn right side out using a bodkin and press.

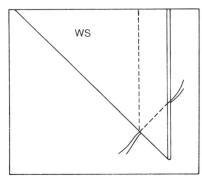

96 *Stitching a corner to form a mitre.*

Elastic Casing at wrist

Adding a bias strip for elastic adds bulk and is awkward to do especially after the seam has been stitched. An alternative is

97 *Making elastic casing above hemline.*

to cut the sleeve 2cm ($^3/_4$in.) longer when cutting out, to include the casing. Fold sleeve right sides together, either before or after stitching the seam, baste below the fold and press the crease. Stitch round the sleeve 1cm ($^3/_8$in.) from the fold. Remove basting, press stitching. Carefully cut through one layer of fabric 5mm ($^1/_4$in.) from the stitching. Press casing flat with narrow raw edge underneath. Stitch again on fold, leaving small gap for threading elastic.

This system is also suitable for cords for bags etc.

An alternative on fine fabrics is to cut the sleeve as normal, then stitch a length of fabric cut from the selvedge at wrist level, right side down to wrong side of sleeve. Press selvedge to cover the raw edge, stitch along selvedge.

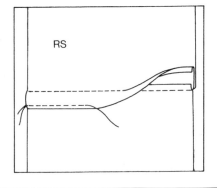

Group Twenty-eight:
Plastic-coated fabrics and leather

PVC, coated cotton, nylon ciré, jersey-backed textured plastic, suede, leather, non-woven suede fabric.

All these materials are flat and hard, even those that are jersey-backed and they suffer permanent marks from pins. Avoid unpicking. Avoid ease and curved seams.

Needle – 90 Leather point needle. Roller foot if dual feed not available.

Stitch – Straight: 4mm long. Zig-zag: 3mm wide, 2mm long.

Thread – Corespun.

Seams – Open: use on heavy plastic, leather and suede. Flatten with fingers, do not press. Seam allowances can be held down with pliable adhesive if necessary. Flat welt: use on all fabrics. On nylon ciré, which frays, it may be best to make conventional fell seams. Edge to edge: use on leather, suede and heavy plastic. Cut edges cleanly and butt them together; join with running zig-zag, darning stitch or any stitch that runs back and forth.

Hems and edges – Narrow hem: fold up edge once and straight stitch or use simple, open, decorative stitch. Wide hems: use Wundaweb if fabric can be pressed, if not, use pliable glue. Avoid facings except on ciré. Ribbing is suitable on all fabrics. If fabrics stick while being sewn or if stitch length varies, rub a little talcum powder over the fabric. Alternatively one drop of oil rubbed on the needle will help. Do not do this on suede or leather as they stain. Avoid basting, use paper clips or basting tape instead. If right-side stitching is troublesome, for instance on the jersey-backed plastics where there is movement in the backing, place a strip of paper on top and sew through that.

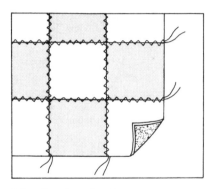

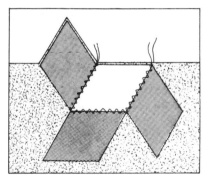

98 *Patchwork using non-woven fabric pressed on to iron-on Vilene.*

99 *Joining diamonds of leather supported with Stitch-n-Tear.*

Non-woven patchwork

Mats, bags, hats and other articles can be made from non-woven fabrics such as Funtex felt and suede fabric. Using a piece of firm iron-on Vilene, adhesive side uppermost, arrange the patchwork pieces on it with clean-cut edges butted together. After arranging the design and checking the edges, press them in place one at a time. Stitch along the joins using a wide zig-zag or triple zig-zag. With random patchwork the article can be cut out after the stitching is complete.

Flat zig-zag seam

Use on non-woven fabrics, hard fabrics such as suede or plastic and fabrics like heavy glace cotton. Fold under the seam allowance of the upper piece eg. yoke. Overlap the edge on to the second piece, both right side up. Baste or hold with basting tape across the seam or under the edge. Using a full-width zig-zag or blind stitch, stitch along the seam with the zig-zag just clearing the folded edge.

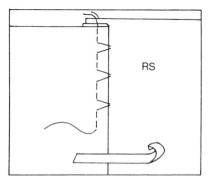

100 *Flat zig-zag seam secured with basting tape.*

Group Twenty-nine: Metal fabrics

Glitter fabric, gold and silver tissue, taffeta, 'toffee paper' fabric.

These fabrics have a high proportion of metal and consequently can be awkward to sew. Fabric may be knitted with the metal thread running through the surface; others may be woven using yarn along the length and metal threads for the weft; some are jacquard weave with floating threads of metal. All fabrics fray because the metal easily slips away from the other yarns. The fabrics snag and the smooth woven fabrics are permanently marked by pins. Unpicking is very difficult.

Needle – 70 Ballpoint. Easily blunted by fabric.

Stitch – Straight: 4mm long. Zig-zag: 3mm wide, 3mm long. Stitching will often be deflected by metal.

Thread – Polyester.

Seams – Open: do not neaten raw edges unless necessary; better to line the garment or bind edges with folded net. Narrow: suitable for all fabrics. Stitch once, trim edges and zig-zag or use open stitch, overlock etc.

Hems and edges – Narrow machined: suitable in some places provided the thread does not show too much (depends on type of fabric and quantity of metal). Deep hems: secure by hand or with Wundaweb. Blind hem: suitable for some fabrics but risk of snagging is increased by the needle piercing the edge of the fold. Facings: thin woven fabrics can be faced with self fabrics, with others use lining.

Glitter shadows
Zig-zag stitch

A style of decoration suitable for transparent fabrics, using scraps of glitter fabric. The latter frays so shapes must be cut to size. Attach Bondaweb and then cut out the motifs or cut the motifs and apply Fray Check to the edges. Place motif underneath fabric and press in place or baste. Using metal thread on the bobbin and very loose bottom tension, thread on the top with slightly tight tension, stitch round each motif with a close zig-zag with fabric wrong side up. Reduce the width of the zig-zag if you can at points of flowers, leaves etc.

Group Thirty: Glitter fabrics

Fabrics with diamanté spots, metal, sequins or decoration on the surface.

These fabrics have a proportion of metal or plastic glitter trimming. They are often knitted with the glitter stuck on with adhesive allowing the fabric to give without losing the decoration. Not difficult to handle but edges will curl up when cut and when right sides are together they cling. Sequins are attached with thread and so fall off cut edges.

Needle – 70 Ballpoint. Easily blunted by decoration.

Stitch – Straight or stretch stitch: 3mm long. Zig-zag: 3mm wide, 2mm long. Stitches may be deflected by decoration.

Thread – Polyester.

Seams – Open: for heavier fabrics. Narrow: suitable for all fabrics. Stitch once, trim and zig-zag or overlock.

Hems and edges – Narrow machined: fabric will stretch when sewn across the width. Place on paper or zig-zag over a thread which can then be drawn up. Wundaweb hem: suitable for medium-weight fabric but test first. Facings: use fabric or lining. Binding: suitable for all fabrics, using contrasting fabric often easier. Difficult to do even topstitching as stitch is deflected by the decoration. Use net and lining to contain sequins. Remove sequins from seam allowances.

Thread fringing

Zig-zag stitch. Fringing foot. The fringe foot is available with many machines, in some cases it is the same foot as used for tailor tacking. The foot has a bar which raises the thread so making a series of loops instead of flat stitches. Fringe can be added to edges of collars etc., worked in circles to make rosettes or stitched in wavy lines to make a haphazard textured surface. Interesting effects can be created with random-dyed threads. It is possible to make a loop pile fabric by working layer upon layer of fringe.

Attach the fringe foot, use zig-zag stitch 1.5mm wide and less than 1mm long. Test the stitch on spare fabric and adjust if necessary. Sew lines of stitching on the fabric, then anchor each one by flattening the fringe to one side and working a line of close zig-zag over the edge to anchor. Alternatively, use a triple straight stitch or embroidery pattern possibly in a different colour. Subsequent rows are worked close and anchored one at a time.

To stitch circles, start at the outside and sew round and round, spiralling towards the centre, change to close zig-zag, flatten fringe to lie outwards and zig-zag round the centre only to finish.

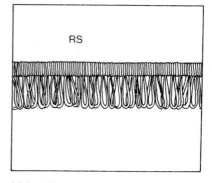

101   *Thread fringing used as an edging.*

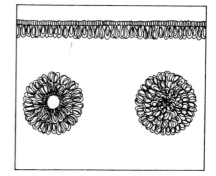

102   *Showing thread fringe lying on fabric, anchored with stitching, and fringe rosettes.*

11

Buying a new Sewing Machine

Although this book is devoted to getting the best from the machine you have I cannot leave it without saying something about buying a new one. Selecting from the range of makes and models available is not easy and an excellent place to start is the consumer reports eg. *Which*, for recommendations on reliability and versatility in the price range you have in mind. One good thing is that the range is so wide you are sure to find a machine to fit your pocket. Bear in mind, though, that you only get what you pay for.

On page 116 you will find a chart showing the most notable sewing features of some of the major machines. In addition, check the obvious things like ease of threading, running noise and above all the weight and general ease of moving it around and setting it up. Compare various machines even if you have a pretty good idea of which one you want. Even when you have decided, shop around for the best bargain. Prices, especially for cash, vary enormously.

Do's and Don'ts

1 Do collect brochures of various makes in the price range you can afford and look through them at home.

2 Do go to a dealer displaying the Sewing Machine Trade Association sign and who stocks a variety of makes.

3 Do take a sewing friend when you go to the shop and take your time trying various machines. Don't be hurried or pushed by the salesman.

4 Do think about it carefully and discuss with experienced friends and teachers, not only various makes but the wide variety of facilities offered by modern machines.

5 Don't let your husband or boy-friend buy a machine for you as a complete surprise. Do let him pay for the machine you choose.

6 Do consider a machine with a handle fixed to the machine itself. It is so much easier to move around and you will make more use of it.

7 Don't buy a machine by mail order unless local maintenance and instruction are guaranteed and you are given an address for both.

8 Do make sure the guarantee is a good one. It is like a new car, you won't believe how quickly 6 or 12 months pass and it is also worth checking out the secondhand value of the machine you are thinking of buying; the best, most reliable makes keep their value.

9 Don't buy in a hurry. Don't hurry over your choice if you are unsure which model to buy. If you are a beginner, borrow a machine for a while until you have mastered the basics of stitching.

10 Do buy a machine with a good, foolproof, built-in buttonhole. Besides straight stitch and zig-zag, it is the one process that everyone needs.

11 Do consider the enormous benefits of free-arm machines for all types of small area stitching. The most convenient machines are those with an accessory box that forms the flat bed but which swings out when the free arm is required.

12 It is a good idea to simply look at various machines in your price bracket on your first trip to the shop and take home some brochures.

13 On your second visit, take some pieces of various fabrics and try the machines for yourself.

14 Do choose a machine with a good range of accessories, extra feet etc., which will add to the range of things you can do with it.

Features

You will want a machine to zig-zag, blindstitch, some sort of overlock, a tricot or honeycomb stitch, a knit stitch and buttonhole. Many machines offer more than one stitch for doing the same job. Some call the stitches by other names eg. honeycomb may be called elastic or smocking stitch. The stitches should be variable in width and length and they should be illustrated, you should not expect to actually work them to see what they look like. Finally, if you can afford a machine in the top bracket consider instead whether you might not find it best to have a more modest sewing machine and buy an overlocker as well. The saving in sewing time is considerable.

Make	Model	General features	Bonus features
Bernina	930	Easy thread. Extra long stitches for basting and topstitching. Thread cutter on needle plate. Foot tap to raise bobbin thread. 20 stitches. Manual thread selection. 4 step buttonhole.	Cut-and-sew attachment. Roller foot available. Pattern matching guide. Knee control – optional. Needle up facility.
	RECORD	As above but without top stitch or needle up facility.	
Elna	5000 COMPUTER	Two sizes of free-arm. Needle up/down facility. Well designed extension table. Clear selector panel. Soft cover for storage. Thread cutter on needle plate.	Several holes to fix circular sewing attachment. Plate for attaching elastic. Extra fine buttonhole. Fagoting plate.
	CARINA SU	Needle up/down facility. Star and hemstitches.	Sideways darning. Good buttonhole foot.
	TX and SP	Basic machines with good range of stitches. Very compact and light.	Same buttonhole foot as above.
			Most models can be fitted with knobs and guides for use by handicapped.
	LOCK L-I	Three thread overlocker.	
Frister & Rossman	LYNX 880 COMPUTER	Push-button selection. Programmed with basic stitches plus cassette for decorative stitches. Digital display.	Alphabet and numerals. Automatic stitch selection and adjustment on feeding in fabric information.
	LYNX 840	Electronic stitch width and length and digital display. Good range of decorative stitches. Needle up/down facility.	
	490	Basic machine. Good range of stitches. Four step buttonhole. Needle up/down.	
			All three have automatic bobbin thread pop-up.

Make	Model	General features	Bonus features
Frister & **Rossman** contd	CUB 5 & 7	Very light and compact basic machines. Simple stitch selection dial. Range of basic stitches. 3 step buttonhole.	
	LOCK 3 & 4 KNIT-lOCKS	Overlocking machines. For normal overlocking but also for seaming knitted garments.	
New **Home**	MEMORY-CRAFT 6000 COMPUTER	Programmed with wide variety of basic and decorative stitches plus memory for own pro-gramming. Alphabet and numbers. Needle up/down.	Clear display panel. Needle threader. Touch only stitch selection. Cross stitch, sand stitch, shading stitch. Punctuation marks.
	SW201BE	Dial selection. Good range of basic stitches plus several decorative.	Clear display panel. Two width free-arm.
	NOVUM 500	Dial selection. Good range of embroidery.	Chain stitch.

Also a range of more basic machines with various features.

Make	Model	General features	Bonus features
	CUMBI 10	Sewing machine and full size overlocker combined. Dial selection. Basic stitches built in.	Commercial over-locking available by turning the machine round.
	LOCK 778	Overlock machine.	Also chain stitch.
Pfaff	1471 CREATIVE COMPUTER	Touch selection. Programmed with 15 basic stitches, 10 embroidery stitches, 17 embroidery designs plus alphabets and numbers. Digital display. Needle up/down.	Dual Feed controls layers also matches plaids and keeps pile seams smooth. Keyhole buttonhole. Hemstitch, cross stitch. Needle threader. Readout button for checking tension etc. Own designs, including sketches and handwriting can be programmed and stored. Bobbin light indicator.

Make	Model	General features	Bonus features
Pfaff contd	1171 TIPTRONIC	Push-button selection of 48 stitches plus 6 embroidery stitches. Needle up/down.	Dual Feed. Needle threader. Buttonhole without turning fabric. Basting stitch. Quiet.
	1147	As above, but without dual feed or needle threader.	
	1035	As above but without embroidery.	
	1119 TIPMATIC	Push-button selection. Basic stitches.	Buttonhole without turning fabric. 6 embroidery stitches.
	1216 & 1217	Dial selection of basic stitches plus push-button for additional basic and embroidery stitches giving wide variety.	Dual feed. Needle threader. Overlocking attachment.
	HOBBY-MATIC & HOBBY RANGE	A range of basic machines with various utility and decorative stitches.	
	CALANDA 791 OVER-LOCKER	Versatile overlocking using four threads or two threads for chainstitch.	
Riccar	SERIES 9600	Needle up/down. Dial selection of 28 basic stitches.	Walking foot attachment.
	3000	Dial selection of range of basic stitches.	
	400	Dial selection of basic and decorative stitches.	
	RICCAR-LOCK	Several models available.	
Singer	SYMPHONIE 300 COMPUTER	Push-button selection. 23 built-in stitches plus cartridges for letters, numbers, motifs.	3 types self-measuring buttonhole. Sews sideways. Audible bleep indicates errors.
	SERENADE SERIES	Dial selection of basic and decorative stitches. Colour coded controls.	Slant needle for good visibility. One step buttonhole.
	SAMBA SERIES	Range of basic machines with various stitches. Dial selection.	Good range of feet. Easy bobbin winding.

Make	Model	General features	Bonus features
Toyota	8900 & 8800	Dial selection, 25 built-in basic stitches.	Colour code for stitch and foot selection. See-through bobbin panel. Flashing light to indicate error.
	7200	Push-button selection. Basic and stretch stitches.	
	7001	Lever selection of a wide range of basic and decorative stitches obtained with drop-in cams.	
	ARTISAN 320	Overlocker. Two or three thread stitching.	
Viking Hu-skvarna	980 COMPUTER	Push-button selection. Programmed with basic stitches, others on cassette. Can be programmed to do up to 52 letters and numbers. Digital display. Automatic needle up.	Alphabet and numerals. Automatic stitch selection and adjustment on feeding in fabric information. Dual position light. Automatic basting.
	960	Similar to 980 but without letters or numbers.	
	940	Push-button selection of good range of basic stitches.	Dual lighting. Buttonholes in 3 widths. Conversion kits available for handicapped, including braille.
	OPTIMA	Range of basic push-button machines with varying ranges of stitches.	

All the machines listed carry the BEAB Kite mark signifying electrical safety. If you prefer any other machine, make sure it is so labelled. Also check the guarantee and see that the instruction book makes sense.

I am grateful to the sewing machine companies who replied to my request and supplied the information from which I compiled the above.

12

Machine Cabinets

There is now a wide range of machine cabinets available. They vary in size, style and capacity and you can choose between modern and period, several wood finishes or plain white.

The improvements made in recent years include drawers and racks fitted with compartments, lift-up flaps, the inclusion of a mirror and various styles of doors some of which are very compact. The machine is raised and lowered by a spring-loaded lever. When it is up, it can either be at full height for using the free arm or lowered and fitted with a perspex or wooden surround shaped for your particular machine.

Some machine companies have their own range of cabinets, others are available in department stores, even by mail order. When you go to buy one take a tape measure with you and check the size with the door open as well as closed.

103 *Cabinet fitted with racks and drawers.*

13

Haberdashery by Post

Items of haberdashery referred to including fabric pen, basting tape, special small scissors and many more items are available from:

> Harlequin
> Unit 25
> Jubilee End
> Lawford
> Manningtree
> Essex
> Telephone: 0206-396167

Send SAE for price list. Also ask for list of sewing books and details of covered button and belt service.

Other books

The Sewing Machine Handbook by Peter Lucking, 1985
B.T. Batsford Ltd.

Choosing a Sewing Machine. Published by the Sewing Machine Trade
Association, Crossways, Church Road, Chelsfield, Kent.

Index

Hartley's, unbleached lawn cotton